I0086536

This belongs to --

The
Winning

B. Kjellberg

The Winning

Copyright © 2014
B. Kjellberg

All Scripture quotations are from the King James Version of the Bible. An attempt has been made in writing to depict evangelical Christian doctrine and practices.

This story is a work of fiction. Names, characters, dialogues and incidents are strictly fictional and are not to be construed as actual, although resembling actual Christian practices. Any resemblance to any person, living or dead, is purely coincidental. Some of the places mentioned are real places and the author has intended to rightly represent them.

ISBN: 978-0-912868-20-2

Available from --

LuLu Press
www.lulu.com

PRINTED IN THE U.S.A.

Dedication

This work is dedicated to my grand-daughter who gave me such expert advice that caused me to make major improvements.

I, also, want to thank my wife who is my main critic and proofreader for her patient uncomplaining help and love for these 60 years. And to all my friends young and old who have read it and made their input.

It is my desire to show, as has successfully happened many times, that marriage is a holy institution initiated by God Himself and it must then be entered into carefully by the Christian. May God bless all who read this.

B. Kjellberg
2016

Moses ... choosing rather to suffer affliction with the people of God, than to enjoy the pleasures of sin for a season.

Hebrews 11:25

The Winning

Chapter 1

"Hey, man, you oughta' get a bigger car," Albert joked as he squeezed in, "it's like bein' packed into a sardine can!"

After a short ride they all piled out and headed for the door. The music was loud and the smoke thick as they walked into The Drunken Zebra Bar (The Stripes, to the regular crowd). Dancers already covered the dance floor, but that did not matter, the morc the merrier, and that was the way they liked it. His friends were already jiving and soon they would be in the swing.

His friend Jim, his closest friend, was a little over six feet tall and average build... brown crew-cut hair. Jim loved to dance and could drink more beer that anyone that Robert knew. Sheila was a very pretty girl if even a little over-stuffed, long medium brown hair loose down her back with a headband to keep it out of her eyes, and bright red lipstick. She was a fun loving girl and she could really cut a number on the dance floor! Her friend was Amanda. A rather tall "Barbie look-a-like" with blond hair in a pony tail, beautiful blue eyes and very shapely, and no end of guys were after her. Once she had a few beers she got quite uninhibited, which could, and at times did, get the group in trouble. They also counted Albert among their five-some. He was very tall and built like a tank – well over 200 pounds of sheer muscle. His hair, unlike Robert's, was rather long and tousled as if he just got out of bed. He once picked a guy up that was bothering the girls and threw him right through a door. Nobody messed with Albert that is why Amanda liked him. These five had packed into Robert's car and planned to have an evening of dance at The Stripes. His car was an older model Ford one where three people could sit in front. The gear shifter was by the steering wheel. This freedom to do as they pleased is what they lived for, so each time they arrived they were pumped up with excitement.

As they entered The Stripes they got their usual table and ordered beers around. Needless to say the walls were painted in black and white stripes. The tabletops looked like zebra skin. Of course, you would need to know where to look to see the walls because the cigarette smoke was so thick. The band was busy pounding out a wild concoction they had composed, while the five worked on their beers and caught up on any news from the two days since they had been together. Albert loved to tell jokes, and as he started they all groaned. "Did you hear the one about this blonde and her husband who were watching TV? The newscaster said that six Brazilians were killed in a skydiving accident. The blonde started crying and said, 'That's horrible!' And her husband said 'Yes, dear, it is, but skydiving is a dangerous sport.' After a few minutes she says to him, 'How many is a brazilian?'" This time it brought howling laughter.

Just then Jim jumped and up and spoke to a girl he had spotted sitting alone at the bar. She was a girl from high school he had not seen in a couple of years. After a long hug and a lot of laughing they decided to dance, since he had finished his third, or was it his fourth beer. This led to Robert and Sheila and Albert

8

and Amanda following Jim's lead and they started swinging. The band was playing a heavy-beat piece they all could really swing to.

Robert was not at all athletic and he kept stepping on Sheila's feet who did her best to keep them out of his way. Any girl who had ever danced with Robert knew to keep her feet out of his way, but this music called for wild and fast paced dancing – a kind of dance that Robert tried his best to do but he almost always made a mess of it.

After several more pauses for beer and the band had started again with music that called for another dance, Robert's feet were getting more out of control with each beer. Sheila was laughing at him so hard that she could hardly keep going, and then it happened. None of them could remember just how it happened, but somehow Robert stumbled – probably tripped himself – and he went headlong careening through all the dancers desperately waving his arms trying to get his balance. He looked like a raging bull – arms and legs flailing wildly. He knocked one girl flying and she landed sprawled on the floor. Meanwhile Robert hit the wall with a loud thud near the band, which, by the way, had stopped and they were all watching this scene unfold in front of them. The beers he had downed did not help him regain his balance, but when he hit the wall he looked around still trying to set himself upright – some guys were helping the girl to her feet. He was thoroughly embarrassed as he mumbled, "Sorry, I tripped!" The girl was not hurt and brushed herself off as she looked with a sour face at this guy who had just knocked her flat. One of her friends said, "I'll teach him a lesson, Terri?"

"No, Wyatt, no! He's just a clumsy klutz!"

Robert was humiliated, but his friends all thought it

was funny, so funny they could not stop laughing.

Back at the table where he had gone to regain his composure, Albert said, "You looked like the drunken Zebra yourself! Plowing through everybody." And that started another round of laughs, but this time Robert joined in imagining what he must have looked like.

Since it was getting late they decided to have an ice cream and go home.

"Jim, you better drive, I don't trust myself," Robert was still feeling a little woozy.

Albert declared loudly, "Amanda and I get the back seat!" they jumped in, slammed the door and locked it. So Sheila sat between Robert and Jim in front. Robert snuggled up with Sheila with his arms wrapped around her and she cuddled up to him – he was glad Jim was driving. Jim's girl was with another group and did not come with them.

* * * * *

The next morning Robert's mother called upstairs to him, "Robert, phone for you, I think it's the museum."

He took a moment to rub his eyes and clear his throat before saying, "Good Morning, Robert Ewing speaking."

"Good morning, Mr. Ewing, this is Rebecca Smith calling from the International Museum of Photography. We would like you to come in for a follow up interview regarding the Assistant Design Director's position. Could you make it tomorrow at, say, 10:00AM? Mr. Samuelson will speak with you."

"Yes, I believe that would be fine. Thank you for calling." he was trying to control his excitement and sound professional.

He had been in Mr. Samuelson's office a week or so earlier for his first interview so he knew where it was and was reasonably calm as he entered the reception area but got tongue-tied when he tried to give his name to Rebecca Smith the secretary. *Did she think I couldn't remember my own name?* He wondered.

An hour later, after much questioning, Mr. Samuelson told his secretary to hold his calls while he showed Mr. Ewing around. He had offered Robert the job and Robert was stunned and mumbled something about considering it, so Mr. Samuelson was trying to impress Robert by briefly showing him the very upscale office and then around the museum. It worked; Robert accepted the job.

"Can you start on Monday or do you have to give notice? The hours are 8:00AM to 5:00PM with an hour for lunch. You can take stock of what tools and supplies we have and give Rebecca a list of anything else you need and I will see that you get it. I will want to brief you on what projects we have in mind... maybe on the following Monday to give you some time to explore around first. Is that agreeable?"

"Monday will be fine Mr. Samuelson. I will be reporting to you, will I"?

"Yes, you will, and by the way I go by 'Sammy' don't be bashful"!

This is what Robert had trained for in college and what he had dreamed of for a long time, and now he had to pinch himself to be sure it was not just imaginary. He couldn't believe he was +actually was going to work for the International Museum of Photography. Of course, he realized that this meant only Friday and Saturday nights to party.

* * * * *

The next Saturday night the five of them agreed to meet at The Stripes again, as usual. Robert was anxious to tell them about his job. He picked the two girls up because they lived closest to him, and Albert picked up Jim. It was a beautiful September evening. The trees were beginning to turn colors, but they had not had a frost yet, so the fall flowers were still brilliant.

Their usual table out near the dance floor was taken already so they had to be satisfied with a large round one in the corner. They ordered a beer for each amidst much greeting and a couple of jokes from Albert.

"Well, guys, I got a big surprise for ya'," Robert began and all eyes turned to him. "I got the big one I wanted! Remember I told ya' I had applied at the photography museum? Well, I started last Monday!" Everyone cheered, except Jim who dropped his head onto his arms on the table and appeared to be crying.

Amanda, who was sitting next to him, put her arm around him and quietly said, "What's wrong, Jim?"

They all fell silent as they stared at him. He did not respond to Amanda's question but just kept quietly crying, his shoulders heaving as he sobbed and seemed be hyperventilating, but no one else spoke – they couldn't. Each one was trying to figure out, in his own way, what Jim's problem was.

Finally, Jim raised his head and cleared his eyes with his sleeve and mumbled, "They killed Billy!" and began to sort of gulp for air. "Billy was all I had," he sobbed. They all knew Billy his older brother. He had enlisted about a year ago and had gotten a place on a top Marine team of sharpshooters. They also knew that Jim's mom had died several months ago from cancer, and he had never seen his dad. It was understandable that he felt devastated and all alone, but why the crying?

"I don't know what I'm going to do!" He squeaked out in a most pitiful tone. "I'm done! I can't take it no more!" and he began to cry again. "Will you guys just leave me? Get outa' here." No one moved, but Amanda kept patting his back until he reached her hand and threw it off. He stopped crying and a hard determined look came on his face and he began fumbling around in his pants pocket and finally pulled a revolver from his pocket and cocked it – it happened so fast none of them could respond – and he put it to his head and just sat there staring at nothing in particular. It caused everyone to be frozen in place; no one could move. They all screamed at once. The girls screaming "NO, JIM!!" And Robert and Albert shouted "Don't do it!" But he sat there his hand shaking almost uncontrollably and gulping air holding the cocked revolver to his head for what seemed an hour – in reality it was only several seconds. The girls dissolved into outright crying, but none of them could move or do anything.

Just then, Jim mumbled, "I can't do it... I'm a chicken!" and threw the revolver to the floor and fainted and fell to the floor. As the revolver hit the floor it fired, which brought the attention of everyone in the bar. The bar tender immediately called the police because of the girls screaming and the shot, and as people surged forward toward the small group someone shouted, "He's got a gun!" and they all stopped and dove for the floor, while Robert and the girls sat – stunned.

For Robert, Sheila, Albert and Amanda everything was going in slow motion. The girls jumped to see if they could help Jim but he was out cold – breathing but not responding and none of them knew what to do. Albert had slumped back in his chair with his eyes closed and unable to move. It was at that moment when the police arrived.

The police cordoned everyone off except the five, which they told to sit down and do not move. About this time Jim began to come to, his eyes flickered open and he looked around and said, "What's going on?" No one answered.

"I don't want any of you to touch anything – girls you can take your bags after we inspect them. I want you all, except this guy on the floor, to go with these officers to one of the cruisers outside. We've got some questions to ask. Larry will you pat the guys down and inspect the girls bags before they leave?"

"You on the floor, stay right there until the ambulance arrives."

"Why call an ambulance, I only fainted?" Jim was totally coherent now.

"We can't take chances. We've got our duty. One of my officers will go with you in the ambulance. Whose revolver is that under the chair?"

Jim wiggled around so he could look and said, "It's mine, sir."

"Ok, don't touch it – we'll get this all sorted out."

———————

Chapter 2

Each one of the four were put into separate cells and were assured they would be soon called for questioning. Meanwhile Jim was taken by ambulance to the hospital to be examined for injuries, but when they heard his story they kept him in a room with an officer there as guard. They said they wanted a psychiatrist to interview him. He was eventually booked for carrying a concealed weapon.

Each one of the four were taken separately into a questioning room and interrogated as to what had happened. The police told them that the fact that each story was essentially the same they would not be booked. It was nearly midnight when the police cruisers dropped them at the bar so they could get their cars.

Albert said he wanted one of the girls to go with him so he would have someone to talk to. Big Albert was rattled and scared. It ended that Sheila went with Robert, and Amanda with Albert, but they were all so shaken they could hardly talk.

The next morning they found that the hospital discharged Jim to the police to be kept in the prison several days at which time a psychiatrist would again interview him and see if he had recovered stability. Jim would be required to go to court because of the revolver, which would not be returned to him, but he still had to answer and was fined for having carried it. This relieved the four but they were still worried about him.

* * * * *

However, this whole episode with Jim really shook Robert up, as his parents had always been warning him; even begging him to end his worldly ways and recommit his life to the Lord Jesus. He had made a good start as a boy, but then college and college friends had turned him away. He used to attend the meetings with his parents until he started college and then he got head strong; thinking he would enjoy the high-life better.

He was completely shaken up and tired. Friday night none of them got any sleep, and Saturday and Sunday all Robert could think about was Jim pointing the gun at his own head. He began thinking about where his own life was going. Were these *friends* doing him any good? Could he continue to use music and entertainment to cover up reality? Is it what he wanted... an empty life with empty friends? His college training had secured him a very respectable job... shouldn't it follow that he become a respectable person? Round and round his thoughts whirled, which kept him from sleep.

Monday morning came and he felt like a limp washcloth, but work was calling him. In fact he had an important meeting with his boss. Last week he was mostly on orientation – finding his way around, but this week he would begin serious work, which he would find out about in this meeting. Yet, every time he had a moment free there was that picture in his mind of Jim with the revolver to his head.

At lunchtime it suddenly occurred to him – what if Jim had shot himself? Where would his soul go? Was he a saved person? *Well, what about myself? Has God given up on me? Was I ever really saved? I always thought so... but was it just my imagination?* He got a little emotional as he thought about this. He remembered his mother and father pleading with him not to get involved with the world's entertainment. They told him these *friends* he claimed to have would just drag him down – but he shrugged it off. He had said, *It's my life and I'll live it the way I want.* Now what he began to realize was that he was the same as his friends. It was like he was on a slippery hill sliding down and he couldn't stop. He could laugh at their dirty jokes, even using God's name in vain was a common thing. *How could I get so far away? I have been telling the same kind of dirty jokes and cursing God just like the others, yet I should have known better. You know what?* He said to himself, *I haven't even prayed for a long, long time. Will God even listen to me?*

By the time he got home that evening, after eating supper at his favorite Chinese restaurant he went directly to his room – so he wouldn't get a lecture from his parents – he was thinking very seriously. *How did I ever get started with these guys? Oh, I think it was Fanci... she was a real doll! Yeah, I really liked her, and then she moved away. That seems like a whole lifetime ago, and here I am now still running around.*

It was at this time that something happened inside Robert's mind, something changed. He couldn't tell what it was but his thoughts changed. Suddenly he began to remember things he had long ago forgotten or *ditched* in his memory. He began to think of all the fun he and Ronald had as boys and then in high school. *I haven't seen Ron for a long time... we used to have a lot of fun. I used to travel around with mom and dad... sure it was to meetings but it was great to meet my distant friends. Now, what have I been doing... drinking beer... laughing... making out with Sheila or some other girl... dancing – in the end what have I got – a friend, of sorts, going to commit suicide. This is horrible. I'll never get that picture of Jim out of my mind. What could I ever say to him, Do as I say, not as I do? Ha! I can't even tell him to get saved... I can't tell him anything, because he would say, You're a hypocrite, you live one way and tell me to do something else! Oh no! Could it be God has given up on me? Did Dad once say that God might give someone up who deliberately turns away from God?*

At this thought he once again become emotional and started to pace around his bedroom – thinking. He knew in the back of his mind he was going the wrong way and yet he was trying to justify what he was doing.

At this moment there was a knock on his door and his mothers voice, "Are you alright? Is everything OK in there?"

"Yes, mom. Everything is fine," and he sat down on his bed.

He was torn between the two. *I've got to stop. I can't go on like this. I can't believe it... 24 years old and besides my job I have nothing else that really matters! This is what I need to do... Get your life together. Settle things with the Lord and your parents right now!*

The next night his mind was still spinning round and round; first one way then another. Back and forth he went, but he did not sleep – again! It seemed to be a duel between the Lord and the Devil in his mind. On the one hand the Devil was saying, *Are you sure you want to give up these friends and all the fun you've been having, and beside, buddy, you aren't such a bad dancer.* But then God was giving him flashbacks to what a satisfying and peaceful life his parents had. God was winning and he was beginning to realize that he did not really have peace inside. When his

18

alarm rang that morning he was finally resolved to talk to his parents that evening. He would eat supper with them, which he had not done for a long time. He decided to tell them everything he had been doing, even about Jim, and get their help to change.

* * * * *

It was his mother's cheerful voice that answered the phone the next morning, and he lost his voice momentarily which took him a bit to compose himself, "Hi, mom! What's for dinner tonight?"

"You mean you're actually going to eat at home?" His mother was pleased, but incredulous.

"Yeah, I want to talk to you and dad."

"Wonderful, what would you like? I've got some steaks, how about that? How about some apple pie, too?" She couldn't help letting her pleasure sound in her voice. *Was the prodigal son finally coming home?*

"Yum, that sounds so good."

"Henry," After hanging up the phone Edith called to her husband who was sitting in the living room, "Robert is coming to supper... he wants to talk."

"Good..." Henry said as he laid aside the newspaper, "I wonder what he has to say now?"

Robert arrived just before six o'clock and both of his parents gave him a warm welcome and a hug. The smell of steak cooking hung in the air like perfume for Robert, and was that apple pie, too? His taste buds were certainly awakened!

After the usual thanksgiving for the meal had been made, his mother brought their hot plates already loaded and they began to eat. His parents asked how his job was going and precisely what project he was working on. His dad was glad to hear about the Stieglitz Photography exhibit since he had seen Mr. Stieglitz once when he came into the lab where he was working at Eastman Kodak.

When they had finished the steak and an excellent piece of apple pie for dessert Robert began with what he wanted to say.

"I said I want to talk and I seriously do; please hear me out. Then I will need your help.

"Last week one of my friends just about committed suicide right in front of all of us at The Drunken Zebra Bar. It really shook me up. He pulled a revolver calmly from his pocket... cocked it..." here Robert had tears running down his cheeks and his voice cracked. "I... can still... see him put that thing..." again a long pause, "to his head... and hold it there... we all screamed, and after what seemed like hours he threw it on the floor and it went off. No one was hurt. What I thought about later was 'Where will he spend eternity?' then I wondered, Why would I think that?"

Robert put his head down and said nothing for a long while and his parents waited for him to get control. "Well," he said wiping his eyes, "it set me to thinking. Where am I going? What am I doing on this road? What do I actually believe? I remember things you taught me. I do remember good times growing up – with Ronald and my other friends, but what could I possibly tell Jim to lift him up? The way I was going all I could say is, 'Here I'll buy you another beer.' Isn't that terrible? That's about all we lived for... the five of us. Forget your troubles and dance your life away!"

Once again it took a bit for him to get control then he asked, "Do you think God would give up on me?

I somehow think I remember Scripture saying that God gave up persons who gave Him up. So, what do you suggest?"

"Oh dear!" exclaimed his mother softly as she put her hands over her mouth. "I didn't know it was so bad. Glad I didn't know."

"Well, son, what is there we can say? The Scripture *does* say, '...*even as they did not like to retain God in their knowledge, God gave them over to a reprobate mind...* that means to go on in a worthless way and unacceptable to God.' Yes, God does let determined people go their way. While you may have done all this that you tell us of; when you were young you were definitely saved by the blood of Jesus and God never gives up someone like that, you are His child. Have you prayed and told the Lord about all this?" His father asked.

"No, I haven't prayed for a very long time – I couldn't."

"I would suggest *we* pray right now. Edith do you have a covering? Rob, I would like you to pray after me if you feel you can."

"Yes, I'll try."

So Henry prayed at length for Robert that he would renew his relationship with the Lord, and with them, and with his previous brethren. Then he prayed for Jim and Robert's other friends that they would be receptive to what Robert would tell them when he tells them of his decision."

Then Robert began to pray, but his voice cracked and he could not speak, and after a long pause he merely squeaked out "Amen."

His father paused with his head bent for a few seconds, when he looked up he said, "Rob, first you should meet your friends... not at a bar, but maybe an ice cream shop – you should treat; and tell them of your convictions and why you will not continue that lifestyle."

"I was already thinking about what I should do. Maybe your prayer just now will give me the courage that I'll need."

Robert's parents were overjoyed at the outcome of their talk and prayed for a long time later that night that he would have the strength to stick with his conviction.

———————

Chapter 3

After speaking with his mother and father Robert began to pray whenever he had a free minute, and he prayed like he never had before. Pouring out his heart to the Lord and depending on Him to help. He was more serious than he had ever been and he felt the Lord Jesus strengthening him and comforting him. He felt a kind of peace that he had never felt before and was sure the Lord had forgiven him. Even then he found every once in a while that he had a hankering to go back and he had to remind himself of what he decided.

After a few phone calls on Friday he met the 'gang' at Al's Creamery. They thought it was funny he wanted to meet there, but a free treat suited everybody. Jim was with them after being released by the police. He still was not his old self, but much more prepared to go forward with his life.

Finally, when Robert was able to get a word in edgewise, as they say, he spoke, "OK, guys I have something to say – please hear me out on this.

"My parents are Christians and I was raised as a Christian. Of course, you all know I have certainly not been living like one, but Jim has changed my life."

Then everyone turned to look at Jim. He threw his hands up and with a shocked expression said, "Hey, I didn't do nothin'."

"What'a ya' mean Christian? We're all Christian... we live in America, don't we?" Albert butted in.

"I don't mean that kind of Christian. What Jim did that night at The Stripes completely changed my life." Rob continued, "That revolver..." as he turned to Jim, "and what you did shocked me. I can't stop thinking about that?" Everyone was silent.

"I have been thinking... 'If Jim died where would he spend eternity?' – it freaked me out and made *me* start to think about myself."

"If there even *is* an eternity?" Jim sneered.

"There absolutely is, but can I continue?" There was a short pause, "I have decided I don't want this lifestyle any more. I still like you guys as I did before. It is nothing (other than what Jim did) that any of you did or said that caused me to rethink my life. And I want to make it clear I don't hate Jim for what he did. Inadvertently he saved me. I don't think any less of any of you than before. I just will not continue living this way. When I was young I trusted Jesus as my Savior, and then I threw His friendship away to do this wild partying, but now I plan to return to Him. That is all I have to say. Thank you all for everything in the last few years, and thank you for hearing me out."

Everyone sat in stunned silence. Finally, it was Amanda that spoke, "Thanks, Robert, for sharing, maybe we all should do some thinking."

Robert hung his head and a tear ran down his cheek as he quietly spoke again, "I care... about all of you and I think... this whole thing was a wakeup call from God... not only for me, but for each of us." He paused as he tried to swallow the lump in his throat before going on, "I feel especially sympathetic for Jim in his situation, but what could I have said to him, or to any of you – nothing! I was running away from God myself. I can't preach at any of you..." After a pause, "Let's keep in touch, but I am not going back like before."

It was a solemn group that went to their cars that night. Robert was trembling but the Lord had given him the strength to say what he did. Over the weekend he thought of things he wished he had said, but he put the matter in the Lord's hands as he prayed. *Help me so I never go back to that life. I want Your help so I can live only for You. Thank You for the job You have given me... I want to use it for You. Help me to not be distracted by the girls as I was. If I am to have a wife lead me to her, or rather lead her to me as You did Eve to Adam. In your name, amen.*

Robert was beside himself all day Saturday. He had always been planning for an evening of carousing, so he prayed a lot and visited with his parents for a long time. He told them about his visit with his four friends. He had truly lost touch with his folks in all this time. He was pleased to find out that his friend, Ronald had married a girl from Chicago and had two small children, and so he was looking forward to a reunion with them.

He had mixed feelings about returning to the meeting, which he had attended long ago... the one which he had turned away from – it seemed like a lifetime ago. But that weekend he went to the meeting and while certain ones were cool toward him, others were quite welcoming – especially Ron. So he began attending the meetings regularly with his parents and speaking with the others about returning. It was not that easy to tell about all his waywardness, but as he did he felt like a large load was lifted off his back, and he began to feel free among them again. Ronald was especially forgiving as he had done a similar thing for a short time and he, too, realized it was not a life with a future. He was happily married and had two wonderful babies.

* * * * *

Months later. . .

Robert found, that he was actually much relieved to be on good terms with the Lord. There was peace deep inside that he now realized he had missed... missed because he was going headlong in rebellion of God and there was no peace in that. He now realized that he had been secretly fearful of God doing something bad to him. It was not an active thought, but just one of those things in the back of his mind.

Soon he was preaching, but it was a different kind of preaching than he had done when he was younger... this time the preacher was one who greatly appreciated the grace of God. Repent and confess your sins – he had been there and done that! Every once in a while he phoned each of his previous friends to see how they were doing, especially Jim. The good news was that Jim had received advancement at work so he was making enough money to keep the apartment and his car and he was going steady with his high school sweetheart. He was doing quite well, but Robert could detect no real Christian experience. The others were doing OK but also had no interest in the Lord.

Whenever Robert thought about it he could see the wisdom in his father's strong suggestion that he witness to the four. He remembered the Scripture that says you believe in your heart, but need to make confession with your mouth. *It actually strengthens you,* he thought.

He was kept very busy at the museum. They were renovating many of the exhibits as well as creating new ones. But he enjoyed his work and put himself into it fully. Deadlines were sometimes hard to meet, but with few exceptions he had met them all. There were various camera exhibits; exhibits on how film was made; how film was processed, and the history of film, especially Kodak. He had always been interested in photography, so this was less like work and more like fun!

After he had completed several display projects he began to experiment with different kinds of lighting for the displays, and in a word getting more creative. There was still the old tried and true standard spot or floodlights, which came in cool white and warm white, but what about other colors, such as daylight, or even candlelight, or UV and on and on it went. What if he had an exhibit that had a very low level light burning continually, and when a person walked up to it the main lights would come on. They already had some exhibits like this but they did not always work so well. As he went home Friday evening he was thinking he should go to the public library and see if they had any material from which he might learn about lights.

Chapter 4

The last thing Robert Ewing needed this Monday morning was to be interrupted by his phone. He had an important meeting in just two hours in which he was to present his newest design to the whole exhibit staff. His design was about a new collection of old photographs the museum acquired and wished to display and he had work yet to do to have his presentation polished. But the phone on his desk was ringing and he had an urge not to answer it, but...

"Good morning, displays department, Robert Ewing speaking," he answered professionally.

"Good morning, Mr. Ewing. This is Terri at the admissions desk calling to tell you a small box was delivered here for you. Would you like to pick it up?"

"Yes, that will be fine. I will be there about lunchtime."

"OK, thanks."

Being twenty-four and un-married, he had not been thinking about girls since Sheila and Amanda and they were not of interest anymore. Sometimes hearing someone's voice on the telephone conveys an image of that person, and somehow this voice got his attention, but he brushed it off as meaningless.

Robert was in charge of making each exhibit functional as well as artistic and appealing. His training at the university had been perfect for this job and he enjoyed being able to express his artistic skills and he enjoyed the challenge.

His recent re-committal to Jesus Christ perhaps gave him focus and desire to perform well in his job. He had also re-connected with the small group of Christians he had turned his back on several years ago. They took no name and had no official pastor. This had become his life again and he filled a responsible place in the meeting. When anyone asked him how their meeting could function without a pastor he liked to explain by quoting what it says in the book of Proverbs, "The locusts have no king, yet go they forth all of them by bands." He was certainly not shy about speaking to others of his Savior. Even now months later the image of Jim about to commit suicide still lingered in his memory. It had shocked him as nothing else ever had.

His meeting and presentation went very well and the others all liked what he had done. This pleased him very much. Some time later, after his meeting, he walked to the front desk where visitors were admitted and was confronted by a most beautiful girl. He wondered if he had ever seen such a beautiful girl. She had long light brown hair hanging down her back and gorgeous brown eyes. Trying to be somewhat of a professional he was not used to being tongue-tied, but for a moment his tongue got all twisted up.

"Uh...hi! Is there someone here named, uh...Terri," He finally managed.

She flashed him a big smile and said, "I'm Terri, what can I do for..." and then something in her froze. She turned with her back to him and shuffled some papers as though she was finishing up something. *Somewhere... somewhere I've seen this guy,* flashed through her mind. "Oh, sorry, I just have to finish up something. Who did you say you were?" But she didn't look up.

Robert thought it was funny that she turned away before he even introduced himself, and then seemed so preoccupied. He picked up a brochure to try to calm his shakiness; "I'm Robert Ewing from displays. You have a parcel for me?"

"Oh, yes, Mr. Ewing," she was glad to not have to look at him, "Yes... yes, I do," as she searched under the counter to retrieve a small box and hand it to him, only briefly looking at him. She was glad at that moment he was reading the brochure. "The guy who brought it in was kinda' mixed up and couldn't find the receiving dock and came here for directions, so since the box was so small I thought it would be all right if I took it. Hope you don't mind?" She tried to only glance at him and moved to get back to work.

"Well... yes..." but he had meant to say, *it's OK but after this you should possibly send it through the proper channels, thanks for your help,* but she was so pretty that he figured he had better get going. "Thanks," was all he could get out, but he stood still looking at the brochure. It was a very good one and he decided to take it with him. As he took a couple steps he realized he had left the box on the counter, so he turned abruptly and nearly stumbled as he picked it up. Terri let out a little snort of a laugh and quickly covered her mouth.

It was then he noticed a young man had walked up behind him. "Oh, excuse me," he said nervously. He was about as tall as Robert but there the similarity ended. He had on a sleeveless T-shirt, which showed off his bulging muscles and tattoos. His black hair hung to his shoulders in clumps. Black stubble covered his cheeks and chin. Robert wondered why a guy like that would want to visit the museum. So he kept watch out of the corner of his eye as he slowly walked away.

"Hey, Terri, how ya doin'"? Her mind was still swirling because of how handsome Mr. Ewing was and still wondering if she had seen him before, when she heard Wyatt's voice she quickly looked up.

Terri sounded a bit embarrassed when she nearly whispered, "Wyatt! What cha' doin' here? I'm at work."

"Yeah, but I just got some big bucks and wonder if we could have a date tonight... you know, a proper date – supper and all. My treat this time."

"You got some money?" She spoke slowly and emphasized each word. "So you held up a bank or what?" She was teasing about the bank thing, but she really was wondering where he got the money. He was forever borrowing.

Robert had stopped walking and was fussing with a display at the end of the counter that was not quite straight so he could hear the conversation.

"Remember that old car sitting in my driveway? Well, some guy paid me a hundred bucks for it – I still can't believe it!"

"Oh! I'll call you after work – stay by the phone then we can talk." A group of people had just walked in and Terri had to turn her attention to them.

"Okey-dokey, babe." Wyatt said as he turned to go. He had to keep her happy because she was the only one in their group of friends that had a steady income. She was very generous and often picked up the tab for drinks.

As for Terri her mind was in a whirl and she nearly made the wrong change for the next customer. His bill came to $18.50 and he handed her a twenty-dollar bill and she, of all things, began counting $18.50 instead of $ 1.50 in change! Fortunately the customer had not seen it, nor had Judy who worked beside her.

"Thank you, sir! You enter through the doors on the right." It seemed her brain was short-circuited. *I've got to get over thinking of Mr. Ewing – he was easy on the eyes, but too... something, I don't know. Have I seen him before, but where? Well, Wyatt is a nice enough guy, but he needs some cleaning up and he needs a job. "No problem," he says, "When I am ready I can get any job I want"! Sure that's what he says, but all he does is borrow. Yeah, I like strong and sexy! No other guys will fool around with me if Wyatt is there... supper sounds good!*

* * * * *

Back at his desk Robert thought, *Something is familiar about her, she sure hangs out with some thugs. It's a shame such a pretty girl would throw her life away with the likes of that guy. Come on, Rob?* He thought to himself. *You see this girl and your mind goes all warm and fuzzy, don't allow that to happen, right now of all times.*

When he got his mind under control he opened the box and it contained several new light units that he purchased to try out as replacements for the lighting in an old display. That settled, he decided to go to lunch. As he walked to the lunchroom he pondered whether the new lights would provide the correct light color tone that he wanted. Some were more blue-white and others a warmer tone. He projected picture after picture in his mind, visions of what the group of old cameras, he was trying to get displayed would look like with different colored lights. Being the kind of artist he was, he was constantly dealing with mental images of his projects.

As he walked into the lunchroom he drew a cup of hot coffee from the coffee machine – added sugar and cream – sat down and opened his salami sandwich. Bowing his head he gave thanks for the food and he proceeded to eat; his mind still on colors of light and kinds of bulbs. Suddenly he thought; *This is my lunch hour... why am I thinking about this stuff? I should read the chapter we will have at the Bible reading tonight.* So he retrieved his Bible from his jacket pocket and as he opened it, it fell open to Job 31 and he saw the words, "I made a covenant with mine eyes; why then should I think upon a maid?" He closed his eyes for a moment and thought; *The Lord is trying to say something to me, isn't He? Thank You, Lord.* He prayed.

About this same time Terri Nash walked into the lunchroom. She saw Mr. Ewing sitting with his eyes closed and his head tipped back a little and a book open in front of him. There had been something about him when she met him earlier that fired her senses. He seemed so different from the guys she hung out with, even Wyatt. He was dressed very professionally and was neat and well groomed. *What's the big deal? He's not my type, but he is handsome, and he looks so familiar!* When he opened his eyes he looked back down at the Bible and didn't even notice her.

Terri's mind took a flip when all of a sudden she remembered... he had knocked her down on the dance floor... *yesss!* She hissed to herself, *I am pretty sure that is him. What book is that? Is that a Bible? No, it can't be... he's not a Bible guy.*

"Ahem!" She said out loud to get his attention and it worked.

He looked up and saw her standing there and said,

"Oh, hi! I… um… was just," and he looked down at his Bible and closed it, "was just eating." And he pushed his sandwich around, "I guess you need to eat too… Just teasing!"

"Do you mind if I sit…" she pointed to the other chair at his table.

"Oh, no problem," all the while he spoke he was so nervous. *Why am I so nervous around this girl?*

She boldly ventured out with, "Have we met before?"

"Hmm… I – I… maybe, but I can't remember where."

"Did you ever go to The Drunken Zebra?"

"Ah!" Recognition suddenly registered on his face and he remembered, "Yes, that was me! I am such a klutz! I hope I didn't hurt you."

"You looked so funny, I couldn't let Wyatt pound you… he offered, you know."

"That guy who came in after me this morning?"

"Yeah."

"Oh, I see," the tone of his voice was dull – unimpressed. "Can I say again, I'm sorry for the knock?"

"Oh, sure. Things happen." She paused a second and said, "Is that book a Bible?" Terri wanted to change the subject, "I didn't think people would just sit and read them."

"I think what you mean is – you didn't think people who get so sloshed on beer and stumble around at "The Stripes" would be caught reading the Bible? I have done a complete 180 turn since then. Let me tell you there is no book like it in the whole world," Robert was getting his voice back.

"Oh no, I didn't mean that, but I'm surprised. I remember my grandma, my mom's mom, reading some fairy tales out of a book and I think she said they were from the Bible. Let me think...it seems this man was caught in a flood and fell into a den of lions and then afterwards he pulled the post out from under a building and it fell on him and he died. That's all I remember of it," she said hoping to change the subject again.

"Well, first let me say, months ago I had a life changing experience at The Stripes and I have rededicated my life to Jesus. One of my friends nearly committed suicide right in front of our whole group."

"Oh, no... I was there that night. The gun actually went off, didn't it?"

"Yeah. He threw it on the floor and it went off. I couldn't help thinking that if he didn't know Jesus as his Savior and he died he would spend eternity in hell. I was raised a Christian until I got into college and then threw it all overboard. But it all came back to me that night."

"So you read your Bible at lunch? If you were just reading it what did you just read?"

"Whoops! When I opened it just now it fell open to this page." He was rather stumped by her bold question. "If you must know here it is" he said as he opened to the book of Job and traced the spot on the page with his finger and read, "'I made a covenant with mine eyes; why then should I think upon a maid?'" He paused a second and noting the perplexed expression on her face he continued, "Well, you wanted to know."

"It seems rather funny that a book that people think is so great actually has stuff like that." She obviously had no use for the Bible, and yet she didn't know anything about it.

"Well, if you must know, it's especially useful information for me right now. When I rededicated my life to God, I asked him to take complete charge even to finding me a wife. That is why I just was praying and asking Him why the Bible opened to that verse. Maybe you should think about God and how you will answer to Him. However, I need to get back to work. It has been nice talking maybe we can continue another time, and anyway I'm sorry for knocking you down." Robert rose and dismissed himself with a friendly wave and a broad smile.

But Terri still had a few minutes and she sat still thinking about what Robert had said, *"useful information for me right now" – what on earth did he mean. It's funny the Bible would say something like 'how should I think on a maid'? Does that mean a cleaning lady? Sure doesn't make sense.*

* * * * *

Robert wondered if Terri had planned to meet him at lunch or if it was a coincidence. Of course, it is bound to happen since they both work in the same place. With his re-conversion he had put himself into the Lord's work as much as he could. He felt really bad because of the way she had spoken of the Bible. It was now very important to him and he truly was offended by her words, but then he thought she might just be ignorant. She evidently knew of the Bible – *could it be that she actually is in need of something which the Bible can give and is not aware of it?*

He had been stuck on that verse in Job his whole lunch hour – *it must be the Lord,* he thought. *I never got turned to the chapter we would have in the Bible reading tonight.* The Lord had interrupted him for a reason. He kept wondering if the Lord was saying here is your work? His thoughts went to the facts; they both work for the same company and she obviously wanted to eat lunch at his table. *There were plenty of other empty tables around, but does that mean she wants to know more, or is she just very forward?* Maybe once she found out about his committal to the Lord Jesus and the Christian fellowship she would look elsewhere. *She's very pretty and is probably used to having guys attracted to her. This is what I'm going to do – I'll make my testimony very clear right away next time we meet up and see what happens.* The more he thought about it, the more determined he became to make his confession to her of his love for Jesus right away. If she was thinking of anything like romance she probably would not want to pursue someone like him. On the other hand, he admitted to himself that she was quite cute.

* * * * *

"Terri!" Judy called all excited, when Terri returned to her desk. She was her co-worker on the admissions desk. "You should have seen the group that just came in. It was a group of nine midgets. They were very nice and polite, but I had never been around really small people before, and they weren't kids. They couldn't see over the counter and because this desk with our computers sticks out in front of us, I couldn't lean over to see them. They had to come around the end. You'll see when they finish going through the museum. I'm going to lunch, see ya'!"

"OK, see ya!" Terri called. *My goodness, I've got more than midgets to think about.* She still could not get Mr. Ewing off her mind. There was some kind of calmness about him, something steady and unexcitable that really appealed to her. Everything else about him was average – average height, weight and... but not average looks, he was very handsome. He was studious looking, but not professor-like or geeky. He had an air about him of knowing where he was going. She realized she did not know any guy like that. The ones she hung out with were pretty much down and outers. Most of them did very little work and then only worked when they needed money, just to get enough to fuel their night's entertainment, and half of the time they were drunk or high on drugs. Of course, there was Wyatt, she had always been sort of sweet on him. He was pretty good-looking when you get beyond all the grunge, even with his shaggy hair and tattoos he was really very macho. On the other hand her life had been pretty empty. The more she thought about it the more she realized that she was always the one treating. She did not really date any of them, just hung out – danced, drank and fooled around. *I guess I hang out with... but they are fun to be with,* she told herself. *Just because you see a guy that is different and... but he is attractive... anyway, maybe the date with Wyatt tonight will get my mind off all this. I am going to get the fun on after work tonight and forget all that talk about the Bible and stuff!* She was definitely mixed up.

———————

CHAPTER 5

After the date went well the night before, Wyatt decided to go for another. "Hello... that you baby?"

She recognized his voice immediately. "Hey! Yeah it's me."

"How about tearin' up the town tonight? That was great last night."

"Ya still got some moola left?"

"Yeah, 'nough for tonight," his voice was a bit slurred, "...you drive?"

"Sure, pick ya up in a few minutes. Where we goin'?"

"The Stripes, then Alex is having a blow-out at his place, his folks are gone. It's gona' be doosey!"

"OK, see ya." She hung up the phone and raced to get into her hot pants and tank top for the evening. It sounded like it would be a fun evening. When she picked him up he was getting a little tipsy after a few beers on top of the cheap whiskey he had been drinking after lunch. But Alex' place was not far from the bar so after a couple beers and rounds of dancing they headed to Alex' home.

"Hey guysh, we're here!" Wyatt loudly slurred as he staggered and nearly knocked over a floor lamp, but the music was so loud that no one heard him, or even noticed. "Baby, let's go up stairs, it's more fun up there."

"Wyatt, I'm NOT going up there!" Terri's voice was firm and loud enough for him to hear.

"Awww! You're a… a…" He slurred out as he literally fell into a chair. His drinks had knocked him out and he lay in the chair with his head lolling to one side drooling on the floor.

Terri had had enough of him so she looked around to see if there was anyone else she knew. She spotted two girls she recognized sitting in the corner on the floor laughing and drinking beer, so she asked, "Can I…?" as she pointed to a place by them.

"Sure! The party is getting a little too out of hand for us. How about you?"

"I came with Wyatt and he's been drinking all day, I guess. He passed out in the chair over there."

She chatted with them for a while – but never did learn their names – she thought the one was Paula. However, the evening was less than fun. She was just about to leave when…

"POLICE!" Shouted a police officer as he stepped through the front door of the Jamison's house, "Everybody FREEZE! Shut that music off!" He was a huge guy and looked like he meant every word he said. Aside into his walkie-talkie he barked, "Pete, are the back and side doors secured?" A faint reply came, "Yes."

"Shut that music off!" He repeated, "Who lives here?"

Alex raised his hand in the back of the room, "I do, sir."

"Ok, you back there, come here, now."

"Do you own this place?"

"No, my parents do, but they are out of town."

"What's wrong with this guy in the chair?" He barked.

Alex had not noticed Wyatt before, "I don't know, I think he's had too much to drink."

"Well never mind, you are under arrest. We are going to book everyone else and then we will tell you what you have to do. Everybody line up here – everybody! I want your full name, address and phone... and no funny stuff."

The room was dead silent as Alex walked forward. "Marvin, will you call for an ambulance and come in here with your booking sheet," the officer said into his walkie-talkie.

Alex was hand cuffed and stood by the front door while everyone gave the officer the information one by one. Each one was given a Breathalyzer test and those that passed were sent home. Terri passed the test but she was shaking so bad that she could hardly give the officer her information. When she got in her car she sat still for a long time because she was shivering so bad. Hot pants and a tank top are not exactly warm, and she was frightened besides. *We were only having fun! I think I did smell pot maybe somebody brought some joints. Could be that's why the police are here. I hope Alex is OK. I wonder if I'll have to go to court... I wonder what they'll do with Wyatt?* These and many more thoughts were tumbling through her mind. She found out later that the ambulance took Wyatt to the hospital for blood tests.

So much for a date with Wyatt: it seems every time I think things will go good, just then they go bad. Why can't we have some good old fun... it always ends like this... do we go too far? Are beer and pot so bad?

What a night it had been and it was really late when Terri got home, but of course, her mother wasn't home anyway... some nights her mother never came home. Oh well, tomorrow was Sunday and Terri could sleep in. She did not have anything she had to do except her laundry and... she thought maybe she should go shopping, and Sunday night she would not party because she wanted to be to work on time on Monday. In the back of her thoughts she kept expecting a call from the police, which kept her on edge.

* * * * *

Sunday dawned cloudy but warm so a shopping trip would be a good way to forget the night before. She had gone through several of the clothing stores downtown without buying anything so she decided to get a coffee before heading home to make supper. Starbucks had some chairs out on the sidewalk and since it was a pleasant day she decided to sit out there and enjoy the fresh air and her cupa' joe. As she sat there she heard someone talking rather loudly on the far corner. There were some people there too. So she thought she would investigate.

Looks like a political rally; why not go have a look. Just might see some famous person. She had to almost push her way through the crowd and as she got through to the front, right there in front of her was Mr. Ewing preaching about Jesus with a Bible open in his hand. She was dumbfounded! He looked right at her as he spoke and a small smile of recognition crossed his face. *Ooops! I'm not sure I want to be here.* So she backed into the crowd as discretely as she could and disappeared, but it was too late he had seen her.

As she hurried home she tried to forget what had happened. What could she say to him if she saw him at work? *Well, I'm going to avoid him at all costs... I definitely do not want to get involved in Bible stuff.* Still some little thing in the back of her mind said,

Could it be worse than last night? Maybe he'll forget he saw me. I'll keep my distance for a while anyway. If it's a nice day tomorrow I'll eat my lunch outside that ought to work.

But when she got home she could not forget the sight of him, and that very rich speaking voice. She wondered why all the crowds were listening to him, was it what he was saying? Or were they just curious like she had been? The only words that she remembered him saying were "Jesus saves" and there was that Bible again. However, those words kept going round and round in her mind. She determined then and there she was not going to let religion into her life – *it will mess everything up.* But at that moment a strange sinking feeling hit her and she remembered last night at the Jamison's...of course, she reasoned, *that had only happened once before. Think of all the exciting good times.* Just then her mind went to the vision of Wyatt laying on the Jamison's chair passed-out and drooling, yuck! *Good times, did I say? Maybe I can talk sense into Wyatt... but he always gets drunk.* Tears pooled in her eyes as she thought of her life. Just then somebody on the TV, which she was not watching said, "...are we having fun yet?" When she heard that her eyes pooled with tears and she shouted at it, No!" *I wish I could say yes, but my life is a mess. I wish I had some really close friend I could talk to. Did I say, friend? Huh! They're all losers.*

* * * * *

Robert often went with Ronald and others from their Christian gathering to preach on a street corner or in a rest home. They each took turns speaking about their Savior and how He died and that sins could be washed away in His blood by believing in Him. Each one only spoke for five minutes or so and tried to appeal to troubled souls to accept Jesus as their personal Savior and enjoy the peace He provides.

He was the third one to speak this Sunday afternoon and once as he turned to speak to others in the crowd he saw the girl from work right in front of him, but when he looked back she was gone. He wondered if he had just imagined it or if she really was there, but he had to keep his train of thought.

On the way home he mentioned it to the men he was with and one of them said he saw a girl sort of break through the crowd and then melt back in but he did not think much of it at the time. The crowd was always surging and changing. Then they wanted to know why he mentioned it and he told them it just seemed rather peculiar – not wanting to talk about Terri.

In a way it rather haunted Robert, how she had appeared and disappeared. He made up his mind he would not let his thoughts run wild, but still there was something about her... He resigned himself to pray about her and for her and ask the Lord why she was on his mind so much. He determined that if or when he had opportunity again he would give her the gospel. This was going to be a touchy situation because she was quite pretty.

———————

Chapter 6

When lunchtime rolled around on Monday it was such a beautiful day he decided to take his lunch outside at the picnic table out there where he could read his new magazine without interruption. As he had done this a few times before, he got his usual cup of coffee from the lunchroom and headed outside. As he stepped outside he could see someone was already sitting at one of the tables with a book propped up reading but he couldn't see their face. Then it dawned on him it was that girl again. *O well, Lord, here we go!*

"Hi! I didn't expect you out here. May I sit here?"

She jumped as he spoke, "Oh! You scared me. Have a seat." She spoke weakly and went back to reading her book.

"Beautiful day!" He exclaimed as he open his lunch bag.

"Uh huh." She mumbled. He couldn't see her face because of the book, but he concluded she did not want to talk, so he sat quiet. He had brought along a recent copy of the magazine "Photography" and began paging through it. An article on outdoor photography caught his eye and he was soon involved in the how-to instruction.

After a short while Terri closed her book and got up and left without a wave or a word. Robert thought, *Ok, if that is the way you want to be, go ahead.*

By Friday they had not spoken, in fact he had not seen her in either the lunchroom or at the picnic table outside. To be truthful he was actually missing their visits, although the conversations had not been all that good. But he thought that deep down she was searching for something, so he decided if she wasn't in the lunchroom he would go looking for her.

* * * * *

For Terri the week had been miserable because she knew she had blown Robert off. It had been bugging Terri and she knew it was her own fault, but she missed Robert's company. She didn't want to admit it, but she liked what he talked about. *I know I decided I would not talk to him any more, but it seems all I think about. The Stripes isn't even fun because of him. I'm going to eat in the lunchroom today; maybe he'll be there.*

Sure enough, he already had his coffee and was beginning to eat when she walked in and he looked up and smiled, so she walked to his table and sat down.

"Sorry about last Monday, but I was in a real funk!" She admitted quickly.

"No offense. How are you today?"

"Better. I really want to talk to you and I don't want to talk to you, all at the same time. I mean I've liked our visits."

"Well, the truth be told, I was missing our visits as well."

"I guess my problem was that I saw you preaching last Sunday on the corner downtown. Do you have to do that? Do you get extra points or something for it?"

"With a Savior like Jesus I love to do it. I wish everyone knew Him. I love to tell people about Him!

No one asked me to do it. No, I don't get points." he spoke with a lot of assurance.

"I was so shocked when I saw it was you that I was embarrassed and left."

"You must have, because you were gone when I looked around again, and then I wondered if I'd imagined it."

"Why... so why would you care?" she asked as she remembered her vow to avoid him.

"Honestly I would have to say I've prayed for you a few times since our visit the other week. I was alarmed and felt almost insulted that someone would think of the Bible as a fairy tale book. Actually, at first I was offended, then I realized that you most likely just did not know how precious a Book it is; I know some people like that."

"I didn't really want to have this conversation that is why I sat outside on Monday. I was hoping to avoid you, quite honestly. My life is wonderful right now," she lied, "I've got friends and we do lots of fun things like dancing, and going to shows, and making out; I don't want religion to mess it up; you know, 'you can't do this and you can't do that'!" she spoke very soberly.

"After I got recovered from my messed up life I just cannot stop telling others about the Man that died for me. It's Jesus, not a religion. Religion can be a hollow prop for people. However, I'd encourage you to have a relationship with Jesus."

"What are you saying? I thought Jesus is the guy they talk about in church. I see His name everywhere at Christmas and Easter. I remember you saying on the street corner 'Jesus saves'. How can anyone have a relationship with Him – He is dead?"

"He's not dead. He did die, but He rose from the dead the third day and after visiting His friends, at one time over 500 saw Him at once, then some saw Him taken up to heaven and He's alive there still. He *is* the only way for you to get to heaven! For salvation you must go directly to Him. You don't go to a church or a priest or a pastor, or even to some other religion... for salvation you speak directly to Him in prayer."

"Huh, that is sure different than I had thought." *I'll have to think about that;* she thought as a puzzled expression swept across her face. "But what about my friends, and my parties and all?"

"Well, your salvation is not based on what friends you have or what you do, it is based on confessing that you realize you are a sinner in need of a savior. You must believe in your heart and confess with your mouth. That is all!"

"Hmmm... I don't know what they would say about that. I'll think about it."

"Well, lunch break is over." Robert said as he stood, "We had better get back, it sure was nice talking with you again today. I would like to continue it another time if you want. I don't believe you ever told me your name."

"It is Terri... Terri Nash. I'll think about what you said. I am sorry I offended you about the Bible." She said as she covered her mouth with her hand to stifle a giggle.

"Terri, I should have remembered. We met on the phone that day. Mine is Robert. I go by Rob. See ya around." And they went their separate ways.

* * * * *

The conversation with Robert was still bugging Terri and caused her to begin thinking about her life as she sat in her bedroom that night. She was born to Kenneth and Muriel Nash nearly twenty-four years ago. Her dad was climbing the corporate ladder at a huge multi-national corporation, and she could not remember that there was ever anything they wanted that they could not buy – money was no object. Then when she was about ten years old she noticed her folks bickering and arguing until her father moved away to New York City. That changed everything for them even though her parents never divorced. Her mother got a good job, which supported she and Terri. She remembers coming home and her mother was never there because she was always working. Terri was lonely and many times scared. She was continually going around and making sure all the windows and doors were locked. In high school then she began getting her girlfriends to come home with her and many times they did sleepovers.

Then she suspected her mother started dating and soon some nights she never came home. By this time she was out of high school and looking for work. She got a part time job as a waitress for a small eatery, which gave her some spending money, but she felt abandoned, let down and hurt. So she started hanging out with some of the regulars she met at the restaurant, going out nights whenever and wherever she wanted. Her mother usually left a generous bit of cash on the kitchen table for food, yet her mother never knew what she did nor seemed to care. When she was home she would holler at her over some insignificant thing, like leaving the basement light on.

All this went through her mind because she found partying was a fun way to forget her home. *My life is going good now... I'll worry about the future when it gets here. Oh yeah, there is that thing with the police.*

I guess I would have heard by now if we have to go to court – I sure hope we don't. Then there is Wyatt... I don't know what to think about him. He is sure fun to be with and definitely very tough and manly until he gets drunk. But... would I want to live with him forever? Having a drunk for a husband... I don't think so! Do I even want to get married? Then there is always this Bible thing hanging over my head... life is so complicated.

Back and forth she went in her thoughts. The more she thought about her life more she realized it was pretty empty. It was actually a shell, masquerading to make her think she was OK when she was not. She wished more than once that she could talk to her mother about life, but she seldom saw her anymore. Still Terri kept coming back in her thoughts to what she loved... guys, music, dancing, and the 'high' that goes with it all.

OK, she thought, *tonight we are all going over to the bar and I am going to really think seriously about what is going on and try to make up my mind. Oh, and one other thing I am going to have a word with Wyatt. He needs to know what I think about him always getting drunk and that I will not sleep with him. I can't believe it that he wanted me to come upstairs at Alex house the other night! Wouldn't that have been cute to have the police come barging in!*

Day after day that week these same thoughts were troubling her. There was something about what Robert said that got her interest, but it didn't fit with her life. She had no mind to change the way she lived, and yet... This was still going through her mind as she changed into her wild clothes for the night and sped off to The Stripes.

* * * * *

Robert went to their weekly Bible reading that evening. They were studying the 4th chapter of Philippians. The chapter is so full of rich thoughts that it got his mind off Terri and work.

On his way home with his parents he had a mental flash back about his conversation with Terri earlier that day. *I suppose she is out with her rowdy gang? Boy, that guy sure looked like a loser.* He couldn't help but feel how empty she was and how much she needed the Savior.

Henry and Edith were older than most when he was born, but Robert at 25 continued to live with them so he could help around the house. With no brothers or sisters it was his job to care for them. Of course, he hoped that when he married he would have his own home; *when I come across the right girl, of course.* The Christian company he met with had fellowship with other companies around the world, so he traveled some, and his parents often entertained visitors from other gatherings. Sometimes he and his parents would drive to gatherings in other cities. There were plenty of young women his age that he could be interested in *but, I don't know, none of them seem just right somehow,* he muttered to himself.

He had grown up in Rochester and went to the Rochester Institute of Technology and it was his training there that got him his present job at the International Museum of Photography at the George Eastman House. He was not interested in art as an abstract expression, but more the design connected with it. Designing exhibits was very fulfilling for him. So far the museum administrators seemed to like his approach to design for which he was thankful. He had already showcased two exhibits of well-known photographers; the photos and some of the equipment they used. The process the old photographers had used to make photos on wet plates intrigued him and he was able to make a display that was much commented on by museum visitors.

Now, two weeks later, he and two others were on their way to a photography show in Los Angeles to set up and "man" a booth for the Museum. It took some intense preparation before he left. The museum already owned the tables and backdrops for the show; and he was hoping everything he shipped would be there when they arrived for the setup.

The weekend in Los Angeles was mediocre as far as the show was concerned. The booth was very busy and he was on his feet almost all day. When he returned home he was dead tired!

And yet there was hardly any time after his Los Angeles trip before he was scheduled to leave again for a special course given by the Smithsonian Institution in Washington, DC, which was about displays and exhibits. This was an intense one-week course. The course was very useful and gave him many new ideas, but it also put him behind in his work at the museum.

He realized the Stieglitz Photo Exhibit was due to open just ten days away on September 14th. Alfred Stieglitz was one of the great photographers of the 1900s and therefore they were expecting a large number of visitors. Since the museum had acquired the rights to show his work, it had to be displayed first class! Robert usually laid out the designs and others built it, and still he had to oversee it.

The Special Exhibits room was a very large and empty room. The visitors would be directed on a path through all the displays and this had to be done in such a way that they would be hardly conscious of the surrounding room and focus on the exhibits.

As he stood looking into this huge room a voice behind him said, "Mr. Ewing, I have the display stands coming up just now, where would you like them."

He turned and saw Manuel from the stock room. "Let me see… just set them along this wall by the door and I will get my layout and chalk mark the floor where they are to be put. Give me a couple of hours and then you guys can begin to set up." The next two hours were spent measuring and marking the floor with chalk and the stock room men began erecting the displays. Then came the electric wiring for individual lights, which spotlighted on certain items. But there were a multitude of other small details before the opening day finally came. There was even a recording of the great photographer's own voice speaking of the story behind several of the photos. Finally, however, it had all come together quite smoothly much to his relief.

Opening day was going to be a real media event, with the Mayor of Rochester present, as well as all the high administration of the museum and the Kodak Company. September 14th was tomorrow and everything must be in perfect order, so Robert walked the "trail" over and over with his notes to make sure it was in readiness. All the behind-the-scenes support – electric cords, display supports, etc. – must be out of sight and functioning perfectly.

On the morning of opening day everything seemed to be working as he had planned, but he still double-checked before the ribbon cutting. To his amazement and pleasure everything performed perfectly. As he was doing his final check he saw Sammy coming down the visitor's trail and he exclaimed, "Well done, Rob.

Everything looks great. Remember the ceremony will be starting in about a half hour."

As he turned he saw his boss with a big smile on his face. "Thank you, Sammy. So far, so good!" He was so pleased with the compliment.

He managed to remain invisible while the festivities were taking place in a small dark corner where he could see what was happening and not be observed. Each celebrity had to make a short speech as well as the local state senator doing a little politicking.

Then during the afternoon all the museum staff had been invited to take the tour so they would be familiar with the exhibit and could inform visitors about it. Even many of the Kodak Company staff were invited to walk through. Robert was on his feet nearly all day making sure nothing went awry. Once the exhibit had been through a whole day then he figured it would be "out of the woods" and he could relax.

That afternoon as he stood in his hiding place he heard some female voices and some giggling as some staff women came through, and when he peeked he saw Terri, but he did not duck back out of sight quick enough and she saw him and made a beeline over to him.

"Rob, this is an excellent job! Did you design all this?" She spoke low but too loud.

"Yep, my blood, sweat and tears!" He whispered.

"Where have you been for the last couple of weeks, I was afraid you had quit," she was whispering too.

"I have been very busy. First, I had a trade show in LA, and then a week long course at the Smithsonian, and then this. I guess they plan on making me work for my wages!" He said with a light laugh. "What about you, how have you been?"

"Oh, so-so!" she said with an expressionless face, "I guess I'm OK."

"Well, I'll see you around once this exhibit proves it won't need me to baby-sit it. The next project is bearing down on me and I have not even started on it." He stepped back into his hiding place as he waved a small wave and she went on with the other girls.

———————

Chapter 7

Terri's evening at The Stripes did not go so well. Several of the guys got into a fight and got kicked out, and Wyatt did his usual thing of trying to sweet-talk her into sleeping with him while he was quite drunk. She was getting fed up with him.

"Wyatt, you idiot! I don't want a drunk in my life."

"Aww! Baby I..." hick "need you." As he reached for a chair to steady himself he missed and almost fell but staggered up again.

"Go find somebody that wants a drunk!" And she turned and walked away.

The evening was young and there were others to dance with so she spent her time dancing and she had a couple of beers. The talk consisted mainly of dirty suggestions and jokes. All in all it really didn't lift her spirits like she hoped it would. However she could not get away from thinking of Robert and the Bible in his hand. *Oh, yes, and that thing about looking on a maid; if that was deliberate it was mean of him! But maybe... just maybe he really thinks that way.*

The more she thought about Robert, even though she was sort of mad at him, she began to want to know more about him. *I guess in a funny sort of way I'm really starting to like him? But I don't like all of his religious stuff... maybe it is just a front. But then... he wouldn't be preaching it on the street corner if he were not really serious about it. I wonder if I could get him to change.* Truth be told she really missed seeing him at work for the past two weeks. Then to spot him so suddenly at the new exhibit made her heart do some flip-flops. Yet, she kept wondering if she really wanted a guy like this – the religion thing kept nagging at her. On one hand she had a drunken guy wanting her; yet on the other hand here was a guy who was stable, unflappable and he had a top job at the museum – what actually was bugging her was that he did not seem the least bit romantically interested in her – she had begun to expect guys to want a date. Was this thing all one sided? Did he already have a girl friend and he had not told her? Maybe he was married. Then why *should* he have told her? They had not talked about that subject anyway. So right then and there she determined, at least to find an opportunity to ask him. *How about asking to meet him somewhere after work?* That's what she would have done with the guys she hung out with, so why not Rob? *I'm goin'a try,* she thought!

* * * * *

As Robert sat at his desk in the afternoon the next Monday after the exhibit had proved it could run by itself, he let out a long sigh and stretched. The exhibit was all working fine and was now turned over fully to the maintenance crew to keep it in shape. It had been a long and tiring few weeks and for a few minutes now he could relax. As he leaned back he shut his eyes and prayed; thanking God for His help through all that he had done, and asking help and wisdom as he finished the week. As he prayed his thoughts turned to Terri, *seems I think of her a lot,* so he asked the Lord to work in her heart so that she might come to a full salvation in Him.

He had not finished his prayer when he heard a light knock on his open office door and when he opened his eyes Terri was standing in the doorway.

"Oh, good afternoon! Come in! You surprised me. I was just praying for you," as he stood to welcome her. "Come and have a seat." He sat and waited for her to be seated. "What brings you here. They must have taken your ball and chain off so you could leave the front desk." He said with a short laugh.

"Hey, I'm doin' fine. Judy was good enough to cover for me for a few minutes. You said, 'praying for me?' why would you do that? I came because I want to talk to you." When he smiled questioningly and started to interrupt she said, "No, seriously... but not now, as I have to get back to the desk. Could we meet after work somewhere to talk? Do you drink coffee? How about Starbucks – my treat?" Well, she was surprised at herself to have said it, but she had learned if you want something you have to go after it yourself.

"Well, let me think... yes, I think that would work. After supper I have prayer meeting but... yes, after work will be fine. The one down on Main Street... is that where you are thinking?"

"Yep! Right after work, say five fifteen? See you there." She said as she rose and left his office.

"OK, I'll see you there." He called after her.

This will be interesting. I don't know where this is going, but I had better slip my Bible in my pocket. A soldier never goes into battle without his armament!

* * * * *

Parking was a pain at Starbucks and Terri had to park over a block away, but when she got out of her car she saw Robert had parked further away and was already walking, so she waited until he caught up with her.

"Fancy meeting you here!" He gave her a broad smile "what a nice surprise. Do you mind if I walk with you Miss?" He said jokingly.

"No one would know that we had planned this, would they?" she giggled.

"This was a great idea! I've been so busy the last two or three weeks that very little in my life could be considered normal. I needed a coffee break."

Just then they arrived at Starbucks and prepared to order. They both wanted the same thing, which made it easy. Robert said, "Two tall mocha lattes, please." And before Terri got out her Starbucks card he had paid.

"Hey, I said I was treating!" she protested.

"Thank you just the same, but I'm enjoying the opportunity to sit and relax." They found two seats outside where they could have a little privacy. "Well, I'm so glad you suggested this. I needed to get my mind off work..." then he paused as they each sipped their coffee. "So what has been going on with you?" Robert inquired.

"Oh, nothing, just the same old stuff. I've not seen my mother in weeks and I really have no close friends." She looked down at her cup so he could not see her pouting mouth. "I told you my life was going fine, but it was a lie."

"What about that guy that came into the museum that time? I think I heard him say something about a date." Robert asked.

"Oh, Wyatt! I've known him since high school. He wants to date me, but he doesn't have a job and he's always getting into trouble and always drunk. I kinda' like him, and I have gone with him on several 'dates', but they usually end in disaster. I just can't make up my mind about him. I get mad at him and then we make up, over and over." The look on her face told Robert she was really quite distressed and Wyatt's friendship didn't help.

"I thought you did a lot of partying – you said something about dancing and movies. Doesn't that cheer you up?"

"Last time we went out to a bar a couple of the guys got into a fight and were thrown out, and..." she let her voice trail off because she did not want to go into detail about Wyatt, "they are not really friends; just people to hang out with and do stuff with."

"Well, the Bible says, 'there is a friend that sticks closer than a brother' and I know that to be true. I am an only child and I've been where you are and now I know the *Friend* the Bible speaks about."

After a brief silence, and a few moments of staring at her cup, she spoke, "Rob, I feel very awkward saying this, but I cannot get our previous visits out of my head. I go over and over what I remember of them." He sat and waited for her to finish. "I don't know what it is, but I keep thinking about you talking about the Bible and Jesus, or whatever. I know I pooh-poohed it because I always thought it was just another moneymaking scheme for the church. I admire the fact that you aren't pushy. I wonder, sometimes, maybe I'm all wrong," she looked up from her coffee cup.

After a thoughtful pause, Robert said, "I dated a girl who was an unbeliever about 3 years ago. We went places and did things I'm ashamed of now. When she moved away I continued the wild lifestyle for a couple of years – you saw me – and then one of the guys nearly committed suicide right at our table. That shook me up and shocked me so much that I did a lot of thinking. Finally, I realized the path I was on was leading nowhere. I admit I had the advantage of being raised right and a few things stuck with me. The result is that God's things became the center of my life and the Bible now provides me with the challenges, encouragement and teaching that guides my path.

"I would guess that the reason you keep remembering our conversations about this is that God may be working in your heart. Could that be?"

"I don't know!" She paused, "Do you remember what you read to me from the Bible that first day about looking on a 'maid'?" She was wondering about her chances with Robert and was genuinely puzzled as well.

"Yes, I do."

"Does that word 'maid' mean a cleaning lady? Or does it mean that you should not be interested in a girl? Can I assume you are not married?"

Robert stifled a laugh at her comment, "No, I am not married, and it doesn't mean that at all, it means an unmarried girl. A few years ago the relationship I had with Fanci was not good, it was pulling me into the world away from God, so that verse is a caution to me. See, I kinda' fell in love with her; we had a class together in college, but I didn't tell her I was a Christian for a long time. In fact I couldn't tell her because I wasn't living like one. We dated for about a year and did everything she liked doing, but fortunately we never got too intimate. I did things then that I realize now were not good, but they led me on a downward path. One bad thing was I hid it all from my parents by lying.

"Fanci was very pretty and nice and I really liked

her, but when I began to look ahead I could see that marriage was out of the question because she was an unbeliever; actually a scoffer – I found this out when I told her of my beliefs; then she flipped out. Same as you said about the Bible and religion. So we both agreed to end our relationship. Soon she moved away and I have not heard from her since.

"I'm sorry for going on so long, but you asked." Robert paused again and they sat in silence for a short while before continuing "I was amazed myself when I opened my Bible that day and it fell open to that page... of all the thousand plus pages, and it would open there! It happened even before you entered the lunchroom. Was God speaking to me or what?" another pause and then... "So after I broke up with Fanci and Jim put the gun to his head... it was then that I decided that I was going to put the matter of my life, including whether I ever get a wife or not into the Lord's hands and trust Him."

"Now I understand a little better about the 'maid' thing. Thank you for being so frank – I appreciate that. I guess, what I really wanted to say was that I want to know more about the Bible. I think there may be something in it that I need and yet I keep thinking... Oh, I don't know... I don't really want to change? The more I think about it, the more I realize my life is spinning out of control and I don't want that either. What do I want? I'm so mixed up. I thought at first of inviting you to spend an evening with me to meet my friends, but I see now that would never work."

Shaking his head, "Most definitely not, unless they want to hear about my Savior!" He paused for a long time and then said, "OK, the very first step is that you need to believe that God exists. That He created the heavens and the earth and mankind. Not just some influence, but a Divine Being, Who is holy and is a Spirit, and He dwells outside all creation, that means anything we can see and beyond – the universe. Yet, He is interested in men (which means male and female) – He is interested in what you and I are talking about now. I spoke to him in prayer before coming… about us being together for coffee, for example."

"You spoke to God? Isn't that what priests are for?"

"They can and should talk to God for themselves, but every person can speak directly to God himself."

"I never knew that, except I have some vague memories of Grandma talking about this, but it went over my head. Mom's mom was a nice lady. We never went to church – we never even talked about it that I can remember. Oh, I guess I figured there must be Something or Someone out there who started the big bang. And here you are telling me you know Him!" Her face began to brighten some as she spoke.

"Do you have a Bible?"

"No." She spoke with a question in her voice, meaning, Why would I?

"Here take mine it is small and you can carry it in your purse. I'll show you where to start reading… right here in chapter 1 of The Gospel of John, put this ribbon there for a marker. The "Word" it talks about in the very first verse is Jesus. The Gospel according to Luke tells the 'Christmas' story details of His birth, but this Gospel emphasizes that He was not just a man, but He was God as well. Read a chapter or two and let me know how you do. I probably should get home to supper now, but we can do this again – if you want. Still my treat!"

"You'll never know how many thoughts are flying around in my head right now. If I want to try to pray what do I do?"

"Why don't we bow our heads and I will pray quietly for us and our visit here?" She nodded her head and bowed it as he spoke very softly, "Lord Jesus, please bless our visit just now. Please bless Terri as she seeks to learn more about You. Help me to guide her in any way You wish – Your will be done. I ask this Lord Jesus in your precious Name, amen."

She was very subdued and thoughtful as he ended praying and he rose to leave. "Actually, I would like to just sit here and look at this book, thanks. See ya tomorrow."

"Yeah, see ya."

———

Chapter 8

Robert spent most of his time praying as he was driving. Praying for himself for wisdom and praying for Terri to repent of her sins and accept Jesus as her Savior. Supper at home that evening was a blur as he told his parents all about Terri and his visits with her. They advised him to be careful because matters of the heart can quickly confuse what he was doing. They were amazed when he told them about his Bible falling open to the chapter in the book of Job. He valued their advice and was renewed in his decision to not become romantically involved because he was sure it would complicate her spiritual journey. The concern was written on their faces, but they stopped short of telling him to not see her.

The next day at work his boss threw another big project at him, which was to be an old time camera exhibit; some of Ansel Adams old equipment. So now he had to buckle down and do some serious work, which Sammy wanted done very soon. He didn't want any interruptions, as he had to keep focused on the project at hand. This would be an interactive exhibit, which required more design work than the earlier one. An old camera had to be modified to provide the visitor with his own photo. For this he would have to enlist some technical help.

For five days he had been on lock-down in his office – he had even worked on Saturday and by Tuesday he thought the end was in sight. The design was coming together quite well, but it was not nearly completed. He suspected he was getting red-eye from working for such long hours on the computer screen. Finally, he decided he needed another Starbucks break to clear his thoughts and he had to admit to himself that at least Terri was someone to talk to – better than going alone. So he walked down to admissions in the middle of the afternoon and asked Terri if she would join him, and she was quite ready to accept the invitation.

"After work, same place?" He said.

"Cool, I'll be there!" she said with her sweetest smile. His heart did a flip-flop.

She had been wondering why she hadn't seen him in the lunchroom. A whole week had passed, but she knew he possibly was on some project. She did not understand his job, so it seemed rather strange that he would get bursts of intense work. However, she had her head full of questions she wanted to ask and she was ready. She had read most of the Gospel of John and some of it puzzled her. So she was looking forward to another visit and hopefully this one could be longer.

* * * * *

It was Tuesday evening and Robert had no meeting that the evening to attend, so he phoned his parents that he might be late. His mother, to whom he spoke, again warned him to be careful and he assured her he would.

Terri was already at Starbucks when he arrived and they even got the same seats they had had before. After the usual pleasantries Robert asked her, "How did you get along with reading the Gospel of John?"

"Well... that's a good question." She hesitated several seconds "Yes, I read most of it, believe it or not! But basically I didn't understand much – well, maybe some. It talks about the 'Word' being *with* God and yet the 'Word' *was* God. What is that all about?" Now Terri was sincere.

"The 'Word' there is Jesus," Robert ventured, "What the Bible says about God involves us believing it without completely understanding it. In the beginning was only God – nothing else, nor no one else. But in His infinite wisdom He has chosen to reveal Himself as three Persons; the Father, the Son and the Holy Spirit. That helps us to understand Him. So first, in order to approach man, He became a man – Jesus (the Son). Jesus was both God and man. Our minds cannot comprehend that but we just must believe it. However, you can see the various sides of Him when you read. For example, He often visited Bethany where there were friends – that was Him as Man; then He turned the water into wine – He was God. Does that help?"

She was puzzled, "Yes, I remember reading those things, but I guess; it's hard to just believe something without knowing why" she observed.

"Well, you do it all the time. Can you see, or do you understand electricity? When you flip the switch on the wall, you expect the light to come on, don't you? When we believe on Him we get a settled peace in our heart that is as sure as the light coming on, because we no longer are trying to comprehend God, but we can put everything into His hands and trust Him to do what is right."

"Ha... never thought of that!" She exclaimed.

"Well, that is called faith. The Bible has a line that I really like, it says, 'Whom having not seen, ye love'. That is, you not only believe but you have a relationship with Him because you get to know Him," Robert explained.

"What about the part in chapter 1 where someone says, 'Behold the Lamb of God, who takes away the sin of the world'? What does that mean?"

"Well, let me go back a bit first. Jesus was born in Bethlehem – you remember the whole Christmas story – He came as a baby into this world to turn the Jewish nation back to God. It's easy to love a baby, right? He had been prophesied in the Old Testament part of the Bible (that's the first half of the Bible) as their Messiah (the Savior), but they would not have Him. Then they crucified Him and He gave up His life saying 'Father, into thy hands I commend my spirit', and in so doing He was, in the eyes of God, a sacrifice. He did not need to die as we do because He was perfect, but when He did die God put on Him the whole matter of sin, which began centuries before in the Garden of Eden.

"When a person comes to realize he is a sinner and claims Jesus as having died as his substitute and confesses his sins and repents of them that person will be washed from his sins in the eyes of God.

"When I accepted Jesus as my Savior I was young, and then as I have told you I became a backslider; I went far away from God. But then I renewed my trust in Him and confessed to him that I wanted to live here for Him. When I first really began to think about what I had been doing and where I was headed it seemed I had a large load on my back. It was that deep in my mind I knew I was doing wrong. However, He hadn't given me up. He took my load off me, praise His name!"

As he looked up from his cup at her he noticed her eyes were wet with unshed tears, but she quickly turned away. She couldn't face him, but she said, "I never heard that before... I never thought that

I was bad; I always thought I lived a pretty clean life. People talk about 'white lies' and little sins and I thought they didn't count. Frankly, I don't know what to say... what can I say?" She paused for a long time after she spoke and Robert waited. Finally, she said, "I read the story of the woman who had five husbands... I have not done that, but I suppose because of my lifestyle I am still a sinner." Now she turned and looked at him – and what a sad look she had!

"I don't think it matters how bad or good we are, or who is the worst sinner or who is not so bad. God is holy and He cannot tolerate even one tiny sin – none at all. This leaves us without any way to escape the final judgment and spending eternity in hell, which is not a pretty thought. We need someone who can save us. Jesus took my sins on Himself when He was on the cross." Now a few tears were running down her cheeks and it seemed her weeping was evidence of what she was feeling deeply.

With a tissue in her hand she stood, and as she mopped her eyes she said, "Rob, I need to go... I want to think alone. Do you mind?"

"No, I don't mind, but will you be alright? Give me your phone and I'll call when you get home just to make sure."

She gave him her phone number and left for her car still mopping her cheeks. Robert felt like giving her a hug but thought better of it. *Even when she cries she is beautiful!* His mother's words were ringing in his ears – "guard your heart." *Well, she needs to work through this on her own, but I think the Lord is working in her heart, praise His name!*

When Robert arrived home he immediately called Terri to make sure she was OK, and obviously by her tone of voice she had been or was crying.

"Are you OK, Terri? I hope I didn't offend you."

"No, it's not that. It is just this whole thing about Jesus that I never knew before. I will read more out of your Bible – where should I read? Do you have a suggestion?" She sobbed.

"As for reading, I would suggest that you read in the Book of Luke – just a few pages before John's Gospel – read chapter 22 to the end. It is about the death of Jesus, and as you read think about the fact that He went there to pay the debt of *your* sins," He paused, then spoke again, "Just remember this is your decision. You will have to accept God's free offer yourself. I hope I have given you the tools to make that decision," He gave her his phone number, "Call me if you like."

She almost whispered into the phone, "OK, thanks."

No sooner than she had hung the phone up and it rang again.

"Hello." *Who would be calling now,* she wondered.

"Hi, babe! How ya' doin'," It was Wyatt's voice. "How about goin' to the 'Stripes' this evening, you need some R&R?"

She had to pause to get her thoughts together – what did she really want? At this point she did not know. Normally she would have jumped at the chance, but...

"Hey! Are you still there?"

"Yeah, I think I better not tonight. I have some things I need to do, like my laundry and all. Thanks, anyway."

"Awww, come on I need some o' your lovin'.'"

"No, don't try talking me into it. I must stay. Thanks, bye." And she hung up the phone without waiting for him to answer.

The rest of the evening she spent reading the chapters Robert suggested. She took her time because Robert's little preaching had somehow touched something deep within her and the call from Wyatt gave her the contrast that she needed and raised the question about which world she really wanted.

She was beginning to remember something that she had buried far back in her mind. And now the thoughts of it began to take shape once again. The time spent, she realized, running with these wild kids was her way of covering it up. She had been... she hated to even form the words in her own mind, but... Oh, it was too horrible to think about. Yet bits and pieces of that memory were coming back to her; an awful memory.

They had gone to visit her Grandpa and Grandma Nash in California; heir to the fortune of the man who founded the Nash Automobile Company. They lived in what she thought was a castle and she remembered being awed by everything about it. It sat high on a hill from which she thought she could see forever, and it had beautiful flower gardens everywhere and even a swimming pool. It was there that this happened.

She remembered her mother telling her once that her father's parents were angry with him for marrying her and that is why they hardly ever visited them. Was it because her mother was not from a wealthy family?

As if you snapped your fingers Terri made her decision. *I am NOT going through with this religious thing. Rob made it very convincing, but it is just too much. Maybe it is OK for someone like him, but not me. I will give him back his Bible first chance I get and tell him, "Thanks, but no thanks!" I don't want to talk about the 'California' thing to him or anybody. Why bother? It will just get me all riled up. It hasn't hurt me all these years; I'll just forget it again and get on with my life. Yeah, I know. Rob is really attractive. Nope, this is the end. I am done!*

The next day was Wednesday and she did not see Robert. It may have been because she did not eat lunch in the lunchroom. She was struggling – she wanted to see him, and she didn't want to see him, but she did not want to admit it. Thursday and Friday and still no Robert. *Well, it's not my job to go find him. I'll wait until Monday. Maybe he's out of town. Has he given up on me? What if he never comes? He can wait for his Bible, but he probably has plenty of Bibles.* She almost got herself talked into going to find him Friday afternoon despite all her resolves. Every time the door behind her opened she jumped; afraid to face him, and yet wanting to see him. On Friday evening she didn't go out with the 'gang' as usual. She sat at home and got herself worked up into a severe headache. Aspirin did not seem to help so she went to bed and wrapped up in all the blankets she could. Sleep finally came.

The next morning as she opened her eyes she thought she could hear Robert's voice saying, "...he gave me peace like I never had before." It was then that she began to realize that she did not have peace. Everything in her life was a big jumble and now this 'California' thing coming back to haunt her. *Can I ever get peace with this thing niggling away at my mind?*

She began to go over all her visits with Robert and see where all this began. That first day when he came to the front desk, and then the lunchroom: the Bible and the verse about the maid: several other lunches: the visits at Starbucks: then she realized it was when he told her of his experience that got this whole thing about sin started in her memory. *Come on, Terri!* She told herself. *Make up your mind. I think this morning everything is much clearer and I feel stronger. It was when Robert began talking about sins and me being a sinner this thing came back to me. I'm sure I'm not at fault. I'm goin'a forget it for good – never think about it again. But shouldn't I settle it in my mind once and for all? But can I really forget I ever knew Rob?*

Back and forth her thoughts flew. *Do I really want to continue with Wyatt and the others? If I continue will it help me to forget "California"? I suppose in a way I have been running from it all this time as if I was to blame. Was I? I never told anyone because I was scared – he scared me. It is just as well I don't remember him; I don't want to remember. Yet, on the other hand, I think I should confess it – but should I tell Robert? He said I could tell Jesus anything. Well, at least I didn't give him back his Bible yet.*

So she tried praying and found how easy it was, even though she did not yet know Jesus as her Savior. That night she prayed until she fell asleep. And suddenly it was morning! She had slept really sound and had no dreams. Sunday dawned bright and sunny and she felt much restored and wondered if her prayer had done that – if God had given her a new start. She decided this morning to move forward cautiously, but she began to think she just might be ready for a complete change – a new Terri Nash.

———————

Chapter 9

As she sat at breakfast that Saturday morning the TV was running the news and they were telling about a car crash on the east side of the city the previous night in which 3 people were killed and 2 were badly injured. When they showed the photos of each person provided by the families – she was stunned, she knew all of them. Wyatt was one of the ones who had died. She was so stunned and horrified that she burst into tears. One moment they had been partying, in fact, she would have been with them except that she had been home waffling back and forth about what to do. The first news reports were that the driver had been drinking. That was nothing new to her, they often would go driving; sometimes they played hide and seek in their cars – driving fast with no lights... *I used to think it was exciting, now I think it was stupid.*

She felt a sudden compelling need to talk to Robert. To pour out her feelings about such a tragedy... would it not have happened if she had been there? Could she have made a difference? Her pleas had never worked before, but then she was in on the fun. *Yes, maybe Rob would have some comforting words. I could tell him just how I feel. He so understands –* yes, she would call him right now. For the moment her shaking from the horrific news had stopped so she dialed his number.

"Good morning, the Ewing residence," a woman said.

"Hi, I... um... I'm Terri Nash and I would like to speak to Robert."

"Oh yes. Hold the phone for a second." She assumed it was his mother. And she could hear a faint "Rob, it's that girl on the phone."

"Hello." came his voice, "Hey, I am glad to hear from you – how are you this morning?"

"I am not so sure... kinda' all over the place. I have just had some horrible news. Some of my old crowd had a bad car accident last night. Did you see it on the news?"

"No, we don't have a TV... You say it was some of your friends? What happened?"

"It is really terrible! Three of the guys I used to hang out with were killed! And two are in the hospital. It has really shaken me up. I could have been with them! Wyatt had asked me for a date..." her voice broke and it took a minute to recover, "...and I refused him. Maybe it would not have happened if I had gone with him – he..." she sobbed, "is dead."

"How awful. Are you OK, or do you want me to come over?"

"No, I'm really shaken up but OK. I would like to talk though."

"How about supper? I will I pick you up about 6:30? You gave me your address when you gave me your phone. Is supper OK?"

"Oh, Rob, that will be wonderful. I'll do my best not to be crying." Whew, she breathed a big sigh as she hung up the phone. Over the last 24 hours her brain had been spinning and then the accident on top of it and now she had felt so unsettled. Just to hear his voice once again confirmed her latest "final" decision.

The rest of the day went by in a blur. She did a little

cleaning, especially of her room, washed the dishes and washed some clothes. Terri finally took a short nap and re-read the chapters in Luke's Gospel. She felt very sad when she read of how they treated Jesus... *and He had not done anything wrong to deserve it.* Yet she had spent her whole life indifferent to it. *I want Rob to tell me more about Jesus. I want to know more. I want to know everything I can about the Bible.*

* * * * *

When 6:30 came she answered the door and there stood a very handsome young man and for a minute she lost her voice. This time she was wishing this was a date.

"Good evening," his deep voice punctured her thoughts, "are you ready to go?"

"I am... I'll just get my purse."

What is it that is so different about her, he wondered, "You look very nice tonight. I hope you are hungry."

He held the car door for her as she got in. "Thanks," she mumbled.

They were silent for a short time as he began to drive. *I suppose this is a little awkward,* he thought, *this not being a proper date and all. She must be wondering.*

"Tell me about your friends. Do you know any more details?"

"It was four of the guys and Mary. I think Wyatt was driving, but the report is he was drunk – any wonder – he was always drunk. I don't know about the others, but they were probably drunk as well. Often when we got tired of dancing we would go play a game with the cars."

Robert was stunned "That's kinda' asking for trouble

isn't it?"

"That was the fun of it – taking a bigger risk every time. Oh, Rob, my head is thumping and I feel so sad. I don't suppose I could have helped, but I wonder..." Terri moaned. "But I said I wanted to talk to you, and I really do. I have been going back and forth about whether I want to learn more of the Bible or not. The way I was living was fun, but now most of those I knew are dead or in the hospital. Last weekend I had made up my mind to give you back your Bible but I didn't see you all week. I don't suppose you ever had that kind of feeling."

"Oh, yes! After Jim I had the same waffling thoughts. The Devil wants you Terri, I am sure of that. Just like he got Wyatt and the others," he thought for a few seconds and then, "I was thinking of the Le Grande Restaurant, how does that sound?"

"Oh, Rob, that is a very fancy place I don't need that!" She exclaimed.

"You are worth more than that; God thinks you are worth more than that, and so do I, but we'll make do with it then." Her heart did several flip-flops when he said that.

* * * * *

It was indeed a very elegant and upscale place. The entry was most impressive with a high, perhaps two story vaulted ceiling and centered in the middle of the floor was a huge bouquet of cut flowers. There was soft background music playing, otherwise the place was quiet. The greeter was dressed in a black tux and bowed he as opened the door and spoke with a French accent, "Bonne soirée, Mademoiselle and Monsieur, welcome to the Le Grande," and indicated with his hand the receptionist who was elegantly dressed in a black dress.

"Do you have a reservation, sir?" She asked politely.

"No." Rob replied.

"Okay..." she looked at her list, "Right this way then," she said as she led the way to a fine, high-backed booth. As it turns out it was excellent for a quiet conversation.

"Wow, this is even nicer than I thought. This is a real treat just being here," Terri enthused.

This has to be a high-class place, she reasoned, *because there are no prices on the menu!* However, money was not a consideration for Robert this time. They discussed the items on the menu and made their choices and placed their order with a waiter who took it by memory. "I will get it right out," he said.

"Before we begin," Robert started, "I want to tell you how terribly sorry I feel for you. It must be a terrible blow to you knowing that your friends suffered such a terrible end. I hardly can appreciate how you must feel. Do you plan to visit those still in the hospital, or go to the funerals?"

"Actually, I don't know. What can I say to them? I don't think I'll go to the funerals, but I will have to think about a hospital visit. The truth be told I hardly knew these people yet I spent considerable time with them. It may sound funny but since I have gotten to know you a little I realize they were hardly friends, if you know what I mean?

"I must say I am realizing more and more how terrible it was of me to scoff when I saw you reading your Bible that first time we met. It was awful and it hurts deep down inside now that I know more about the Bible. What you said last visit... I guess it was just... oh, well, I can't remember... but it seems like a year ago... about me confessing my sins. It has caused me to think deeply and I suddenly recalled something that happened when I was about 6 or 7 years old that I have not thought about, or rather I kept buried for years. I am quite sure I was not at fault, but I think I should deal with it and leave it." She paused for a long time, and her eyes filled with tears and Robert waited for her to continue.

"It happened when we visited my grandparents in California... I can remember every detail, but I can't remember the man." As she blurted it out the tears began rolling down her cheeks.

"How awful! You mean he... oh, no!" Robert was shocked, and this time he reached, instinctively for her hand, "You don't remember the man?"

"No," she managed to say as she sobbed, "I can't... remember him. Maybe it is just as well."

"I think so. God does not hold children accountable for their sins, even if they are to blame, until they are older and you probably could not have done anything about it anyway. However, I believe this is a clear sign that God is working in your heart. He wants everything clear with you. Have you prayed?"

Her tears had stopped and she wiped the remainder away with a tissue. "I tried, but I have never really told Jesus that I want Him for my Savior; it seems like a step too big to take. I feel like I don't know anything about the Bible, or about Him. I cannot quite understand why I need to accept Him as my Savior if His death was for all. Doesn't that mean the sins of everyone are gone?" She now lifted her eyes away from the table and looked at Robert.

Robert paused for a few moments before he said, "Do

you remember the recent ferry boat that collapsed in the Bay of Bengal or somewhere?" and she nodded; "Suppose a rescue boat came along and saw those people in the sea and threw a rope to them. The rescuers were sent for them all, but only the ones who took hold of the rope would be saved – the rest would drown. That is how it is. Will you take hold of the rope?"

She sat with her head down for a very long time. Robert prayed as he waited because he knew that this was the moment when she would sink or be saved. Finally, she looked up wiping tears from her eyes and beamed him a smile and she said, "I think I've got hold of it! I have this satisfied feeling. I just said to Jesus that I want Him as my Savior. I feel at peace… and it is wonderful… Rob this is wonderful. Just let me bow my head and enjoy this for a few moments."

Robert, too, bowed his head still holding her hand and he began to pray aloud softly. *Lord Jesus, please fill Terri's heart with your love. Hold her in your arms, comfort her even in her loss of her friends and give her new friends – real friends, and be her Friend. Help her to tell others of You. In Your name, Lord Jesus, I ask it, Amen.*

Terri looked up when he said "Amen," now she was smiling. "This is so wonderful, Rob, I don't know how to thank you for helping me." She got up and came to him and hugged him. It was just a quick hug, but it astonished him. The evening finished in one of rejoicing for both of them. Robert was filled with joy and he knew heaven would be.

———————

Chapter 10

Robert ate lunch at his desk on Monday and continued working on the old cameras project. As he worked there was a light knock on the door and he called for the knocker to come in. In stepped Terri, "Hi, I thought you would be eating in here, can I join you?"

"Sure! I should have taken a break, but you know how it is... when I get going on a project one thing leads to another." They continued to exchange pleasantries.

She sat quiet for a while, obviously thinking.

Robert waited for her.

Finally, she said, "This seems so soon and yet sometimes I wish I could go back and hear the music and do some dancing," she had a wistful look, "it really was fun. You know last Friday night I had a huge battle in my mind... do I or don't I want to accept Jesus as my Savior. And it still keeps coming up. It seems I may be missing out on the fun. And yet... I don't know..." she let her voice trail off.

Robert, again, waited for her to finish.

"We used to have so much fun, but sometimes things went bad. I guess what I am saying is, I would kinda' like to go back and see. Can't a believer in Jesus dance and listen to that music? Don't Christians sometimes drink beer? Do you ever drink beer?"

"Yes, sometimes I'll have a beer with pizza." He paused, and then with a smile said, "You know, Terri, you were the one who wanted to know about the Bible and Jesus. You don't owe me anything; you can do as you wish. Only, I won't go along with ya."

"I know... I know... and yet I feel like I am changing too fast. That feeling of peace and love I had in the restaurant the other night was very real. I don't ever want it to go away. I just don't know if I can live the way you do."

"Well, in that case, maybe you should go back and see what it was like. There are people who are saved – backsliders – who go back into the world, but they lose the enjoyment that could have been theirs. Just remember, the Devil is already working to destroy the enjoyment of your salvation," Robert felt sick in his heart.

"If I do it, I hope I will not offend you. I do think I should be sure. I really did like the music and dancing. Do you think I could continue in my commitment to the Lord and still go on with the music and dancing?"

"Do you mean you want both worlds? Well, there is a warning in Scripture, *'whosoever therefore will be a friend of the world is the enemy of God.'*"

"Ouch! That's pretty clear. I'll tell you what; I will go just tonight and put it to the test. I'll go to The Stripes where we always hung out and see."

"I will pray that the Lord will be with you and open your eyes. I sincerely doubt that you will like it."

That Monday night when she walked into The Stripes the music was blaring and the laughing and shouting was loud. She stood at the door for a moment to adjust to it all, and suddenly out of the crowd Mike appeared and sauntered up to her.

"Hey, Terri, where you been we been missing ya'. How about a dance?"

"Oh I've been around. Yeah, I'll take the dance."

And away she went as if nothing had happened, but her brain was spinning. Something deep within her was crying out "this is wrong"! Just then somebody bumped into them and Mike let loose with a stream of profanity, cursing the person who bumped him – he was using the name of Jesus. She pushed away from him and when he registered a complaint for what she had done, she quietly said, "That is my Savior you're talking about."

Mike looked at her in shock and then fairly bellowed, "So you've gone religious have you. Hey, did you all hear that? Terri's gone religious." But he said it to her back as she was walking out the door. She sat in her car and wept for a long time before she could go home. Robert was right – she had changed, the others hadn't!

* * * * *

She could not face Robert, so it wasn't until the next Monday that she met him in the lunchroom. She meekly pulled out the other chair at his table and sat down without saying a word. Robert looked up and said nothing, but smiled as if to welcome her.

She started to say something, but broke down in tears, which took a few moments to control. "Rob," she sniffed "you were right. It wasn't the same, or rather, it *was* the same and *I* wasn't the same. They made fun of me when I told Mike he was using my Savior's name. A month ago I would have just laughed at him. Now I'm done with that life – completely done with it," she had brightened as she spoke with new resolves.

"At least now you settled your curiosity. I am sure the Lord Jesus appreciated your confession! Who knows maybe Mike will think about what you said someday." Robert was very encouraged.

After a few moments of quiet Terri spoke again, "Do you think I could come to at least one of your meetings sometime?"

"Absolutely, I would be pleased if you would."

"When?"

"Tonight is prayer meeting; Thursday night is the Bible reading; and on Sunday there are 3 meetings. You are welcome at any or all."

"How about starting tonight, is that OK. I am really excited about this. Would you pick me up so I can see where to go when I come by myself?"

"Sure, that way you can meet my folks. I'll be at your house at just about 7:00, is that OK."

"I'll be ready."

Then they finished their lunches as Robert asked how admissions to the museum were going, and were they getting a lot of visitors? She reminisced about the troop of midgets that had come as well as other unusual visitors. He was interested and amused by what went on at the front desk.

They walked to his office and he showed her his design for the camera exhibit; he showed her the ancient camera that was modified so the visitor could press a button and the camera would take a picture of the visitor and print it out so the visitor could have it. The picture had to be black and white as well as a little blurry by modern standards. "Like those things in the mall where you can take your own picture." She was getting the idea of it and was intrigued by it. She told him she had done a lot of art in high school and really liked it, so seeing his designs fascinated her. This lunch period had gone by swiftly.

* * * * *

That evening Robert opened the rear car door and Terri quickly slid in with a "Good evening!" to Robert's parents.

"Good evening," his mother and father spoke at once.

"I am excited about this privilege of being allowed to visit your meeting," Terri enthused.

Mr. Ewing began, "So we also are pleased that you wanted to come. Robert has told us about your many visits, and we would like to get to know you ourselves."

"Our Robert," his mother was proud of him "loves to speak to others about the Lord Jesus, so when he told us of you we were not surprised," his mother was sounding unworried and stretching the truth a bit.

"I must admit this evening I am a little apprehensive and... maybe a little scared," Terri spoke quietly.

"What was that?" Mr. Ewing was a little hard of hearing, "I didn't hear what you said," as he tilted his head back over the front seat.

"I was just saying, Mr. Ewing, that I'm a little scared."

"Oh, don't be scared! Nobody there will bite you! We welcome visitors." Under his breath he said "most of us."

"It certainly is going to be exciting for me, I can't remember ever being in a church."

"Well, this won't look much like a church, just a little meeting hall," Mrs. Ewing filled in.

"We're just about there," Robert stated, "You can sit with my mother. All you will need tonight is a Hymn Book and I'll get you one. So calm your nerves and enjoy!"

His parents were so kind, and yet it was all so new. But she did really feel deep in her heart that God had forgiven her and that Jesus had already become precious to her despite what Mike or any of the others would say.

Just then they pulled into a tiny parking lot next to a plain little building, no stained glass windows nor elaborate carvings. She saw a sign on the front but did not have time to read it – she would later. A nicely dressed man and woman were just going into the building and she noticed the woman was wearing a dress and had a large rather droopy hat on. *Do they have a dress code,* she wondered? She had not thought about how to dress and Robert had said nothing so she decided she would put this on her question list. Soon they four were walking into the meeting room. Robert walked with his father to avoid any suggestion or inference others might make. After all she was just his co-worker.

The room they walked into was very plain but clean and had two circles of folding chairs one outside the other. Robert reached to a small table by the door and picked up a book and gave it to Terri. Then she followed his mother to a seat in the second row, while Robert and his father sat in front.

As she sat there watching as others came in, a husband and wife with a child about 2 years old entered, and her heart did a flip when she realized it was Ronald who was one of the kids she hung out with after high school. *Ronald... married and with a kid... wow! Whatever is he doing here? Well, whatever am I doing here?* She was stunned! After he sat down next to Robert he looked over at her and his face registered astonishment and surprise. There was no doubt he recognized her.

She remembered that he had quit coming with them, but she never heard why. Then she thought back to a time 5 years ago when they all had too much to drink. She got so sick she vomited all over Ronald as he held her in his arms. They had been kissing and hugging, but suddenly the world began to spin and she got really sick. Poor Ron! She remembered feeling so helpless, and he was very grossed out by it. Then when he jumped up she remembered he was so drunk himself he slipped and fell into her lap – worse yet!

She had kinda' liked him then, and now she knew why that was. He had been raised in a Christian home and probably had the same values that Robert had. *This is going to be awkward! Real awkward! What can I say to him? I can't say, "How did you get here? Nor, "Wow, I am surprised to see you!" He will say the same. I think I will say, "I am very happy to see you, Ron." Well, I should focus on the meeting, although I can't avoid seeing him sitting there.* This was so strange! First of all for her to even come to a church meeting, and then to see one of the old gang... she felt out of place and at home all at the same time.

They all waited while other folks arrived and took their seats, and finally when the clock showed 7:30 Ronald said, "Could we sing number fifteen?" At that every one opened their Hymn Books to number 15, so Terri followed along. Someone led out with singing and soon everyone was singing together. In a way it was beautiful as they all sang in unison, "Lord on the throne Thy love's the same, as once upon the cross of shame..." Those were words that she could understand even though she did not know the tune.

She thought the singing was almost divine, there were no instruments and yet they all sang together – there was not even a song director! After the song there was a short period of quiet until one of the men got to his feet and closing his eyes he began to speak to God. At the same time everyone else bowed their heads and it looked like they closed their eyes – except Terri because she wanted to see what was going on.

One after the other the men prayed. Robert even prayed and she paid close attention to his every word. *This sure is a good lesson in how to pray,* she thought; *they speak directly to God. Also, they are sincere in what they ask of Him – not for themselves, but for others. They even seem to know the ones they pray for. This is wonderful! I wonder if the ladies get to pray too?*

After the men had prayed, another hymn was given out and sung, and then the meeting was over. Actually, she was so involved with what was said and what was happening she thought the meeting went by too fast. Soon everyone was milling around, she had not counted but she guessed there were maybe 20-25 people. They all came over and shook her hand and asked her name and told her theirs, which she couldn't remember. Most of them said they were very pleased to see her, or pleased that she had come – something like that.

And then suddenly Ronald stood in front of her. "Ron," she gasped, "I had no idea you would be here."

"I was shocked when I sat down and saw you sitting there. I had to pinch myself to make sure I wasn't dreaming. Have you been converted then?"

"Oh yes, I took Jesus as my Savior. Of course, I never held a Bible until Robert gave me his about a month ago, so I still have a long way to go. The Ewings have been so kind to me. I work with Robert out at the film museum that's how I got to know about Jesus."

"Well, you are going to have to come over to the house for a meal sometime. Alyssa, my wife, is from Chicago and we have Peter who will soon be two. I'll see what will work out as far as time and all."

"I would love that. See ya!"

When they got in the car to go home to the Ewing's, Robert was curious, "How did you know Ronald?"

"We went to high school together and he hung out with the rest of us for several years. He was one of the more decent guys he seemed to be different than the others. Now I know why, he had good parents."

"He was a great trial to his parents for those years." Robert's father put in, "his mother was really down in the dumps for a long time after he started to run around. It was truly remarkable how he suddenly made a complete turn. We were all rejoicing about it, and then when he took up courting Alyssa his folks were 'over the top'. She was one of the most sensible young women in the Chicago gathering."

"Well, he wants me to come for dinner sometime and I would like that. It will be interesting to hear his story."

Soon they were at the Ewing's house – another new experience for her. She had never visited there before. His parents welcomed her into the house and after some more chitchat his mother announced that the pie was ready, "Come and get it!" So they sat at the table in the kitchen and after his father gave thanks they began to eat – and was it ever so good!

"So, Terri, what did you think about the prayer meeting?" Henry asked.

She blushed a little feeling self-conscious and said, "It was a completely new experience... I mean completely! I think I learned how to pray from listening. My prayers were very crude compared to what I heard."

"God loves to hear any sincere prayer, no matter how crude." She was beginning to see where Robert got his kind and even affectionate way. They chatted about her job at the museum, and about her parents and her living arrangements. They shared with her about some of the meetings they had visited. They talked more about Ronald's wife and how they had gone to the wedding in Chicago and got to see the city. Robert had not gone to the wedding because he was still running wild. The evening went by far too fast, but she excused herself saying she needed to do some things at home before bed.

"What a wonderful evening. Thank you Mr. & Mrs. Ewing so much."

"What about having supper here on Wednesday night?" Robert's mother asked.

"Oh, I would love that, but don't go to a lot of trouble for me." Terri sounded delighted, "supper for me is usually pretty skimpy."

All the way home she was bubbling with the wonderful experience of the evening, and how nice his parents were, and how nice the people at the meeting were, and on and on. When they arrived at her home, Robert walked her to the door and she thanked him very warmly as he took her hand and held it for a moment, and then turning he went to the car.

Chapter 11

"Hey, Terri," her work partner said as she approached her work station at the admissions desk the next morning, "how's it goin' with your love affair?"

"Mornin', Judy!" Terri said as she turned her computer on, "I didn't know I had a 'love affair'..." she paused as the screen came up and she clicked to the needed program. "If it's any of your business... I have found a new life."

"Wow! Is he that glamorous that he changes everything?"

"No, it isn't him," she paused as she checked the ticket printer to make sure it was loaded. "I might as well tell you – I have given my life to Jesus. I have real peace that I never knew existed before, and Mr. Ewing," she deliberately used his full name, "has helped me find it. Judy, I can't tell you how wonderful it is."

"Oh no, you've gone religious! I can't believe it!" Exclaimed Judy.

"No, I have not 'gone religious'. I am beginning to know Jesus – you know, the 'Christmas' Jesus. He is wonderful! You should ask Mr. Ewing to help you know Him too."

"Huh, not me. I've already got a life and I don't need it changed." Judy almost scoffed as she said it.

"OK, gotta' go!" As the first visitors arrived Terri turned away from Judy, "Good morning, how can I help you?"

"Good morning," obviously the father of the family

said, "we would like 4 adult and 2 child tickets to the general museum, please."

"Would you also like tickets to the Alfred Stieglitz Photos Exhibit? They are $5.00 for each person over 12 years old – under 12 are free."

"No, thank you, I think just the general museum."

So Terri swiped the customer's credit card and the computer printed out the needed tickets and the family walked toward the entrance guard who took their tickets. The day at the museum had started and Terri felt it was like her life – it had just begun. Yet, the conversation with Judy really troubled her, but she remembered what she was like not that many days ago, when she had been so disrespectful of Robert reading his Bible – *the very same Bible I now carry in my purse!*

Next a busload of seventh and eighth grade students came in. What a lot of noise and commotion that was! There were three parents in charge – at least they wanted to be in charge, but they took care to get everyone tickets. They wanted to go to the Stieglitz exhibit as well. Terri and Judy both worked to get the tickets printed out and the tour on its way.

"Whew! That was over the top noise!" Judy exclaimed.

"You can say that again! How are they going to herd those kids through without losing a few?" Terri wondered.

"Oh well," Judy sighed, "that's a day in the life of a museum."

* * * * *

Wednesday crept by minute by minute because Terri was so looking forward to dinner with Robert's folks.

She really enjoyed being with them on Monday night. Unflustered and unexcitable seemed to be family traits, but then she wondered if it was not really a Christian characteristic. Somewhere along the way she had remembered Robert saying that the word 'Christian' means 'Christ like'.

She did not dare to compare them to her own parents. For the last few years she felt like she hardly had any parents. *If dad is mad at mom, at least he could come and say hello to me, for Pete's sake! I wonder what he looks like after all these years, maybe he's bald and don't want me to see him that way. And then there is always mom... she is supposed to be living with me, but who knows where she is I seldom see her. Oh sure, she would say she wants to be a good example for her daughter! Well, I can tell her a few things next time I see her! I'm only her daughter by blood.*

Robert's parents appeared to be much older than Terri's mom. She supposed they were older when they married – maybe Robert has that gene too. *I do think some weird things, don't I? Nevertheless, I have a million questions to ask them. What I ought to do is write them down so I don't forget.* So, since the visitors arriving to the museum had slowed down, she began a list:

- Is there a dress code for the meetings?

- Why do only the men speak?

- What about the Holy Spirit that Robert mentioned?

Her 'million of questions' ended with just three. She thought maybe that was enough for now... and then she remembered she also wanted to know if she could attend other meetings; and would it be OK if she drove her own car.

When the museum closed for the night she quickly finalized her records and closed her computer down, said goodnight to Judy and hustled off for home and a shower and change of clothes. Mrs. Ewing had not named a time so once she was cleaned up she jumped into her car and was on her way.

"Good evening, Terri," Mrs. Ewing said as she opened the door, "Come on in. How are you this evening?"

"I am just fine and I am excited about being with you and Mr. Ewing and I am full of questions."

"Well, we are not great question answerers, but we will sure try."

"Will Robert be here?" She was really hoping he would be, "I didn't see him today."

"No, actually he got sent to New York City because of some exhibit he is working on, he plans to be home by Friday night."

"Then I will have you and Mr. Ewing all to myself," she chose to look at the bright side.

While Mrs. Ewing finished up the meal she stood in the kitchen visiting with her. She found that they had indeed married when they were in their middle 30's. Mr. Ewing had gone to grad school and then did some specialization, which took more studies and he wanted to wait until his schooling was over, "and I was apparently the girl that the Lord had waiting for him. At least, that's the way I like to think of it," his mother said.

Soon Mr. Ewing was roused from a nap when his wife called that supper was ready. He was very pleased to see Terri there apparently he had forgotten she was coming. "Here I had forgotten you were coming. It's a little quiet around here when it is just the two of us so we welcome visitors." he said, which pleased

94

Terri. As the meal progressed Terri said she had written down some questions she wanted to ask, but forgot the paper at work! But she thought she could remember, as there were only three or four.

"The one thing I wondered about was whether you have a dress code for your meetings?" she ventured right away after they began to eat.

"No, there is no dress code, except for a couple things – respect being the most important; we regard ourselves as meeting with Jesus; a very great personage. First of all, did you read 1 Corinthians 11 where it speaks about a woman having her head covered when she prays? That is why the women wear a head covering in the meeting, and they also cover their heads when we pray at home.

"I see you wear pants or slacks sometimes, which we view as a mark of the world since it began with the women's equality movement. We don't feel that they are proper attire in our meetings. Some specific activities may require them for modesty, of course, like cycling or hiking and so forth.

"A woman who is filling out her place as outlined by God in Scripture is doing something a man cannot do, and there is glory attached to it."

"Yes, Rob suggested I read 1 Corinthians 11 and I did," then she paused for a minute, "I guess I should read it over again," another pause... "However, later in that chapter it speaks about the bread and cup. What is that about?"

"Before Jesus was crucified He asked His disciples to remember Him after He had ascended. You can read about it in Luke 22 about verse 18 or 19. If you come to the meeting on Sunday, we call it the Lord's Day, you will see how we remember Him."

So they talked much later than any of them had thought they would, but Terri was filled with new knowledge and she was thrilled that she had been invited for the meal and visit, even though she did not ask all her questions.

"I want to thank you both so much. This evening has meant a lot to me and I am stuffed with both food and new thoughts."

"Pray about this Terri, I am sure the Lord will help you understand. Also, I want you to know that we are here for you if ever you just want to drop in, or phone with a question. Our Christian group may seem rather odd from the viewpoint of someone like yourself, but the Bible is our textbook and the Lord Jesus is our object and model." Both of them gave her a hug, and she was on her way home after a fun and interesting evening.

As she got ready for bed she thought of her friends, so-called, that had died in the car crash. Had any of them ever met Jesus Christ? Had any of them been saved? How awful to think of going into eternity without Jesus! She was again so thankful God had allowed her to live and to become a believer in Jesus. So she made up her mind to go to the hospital and see Dale and Eric, maybe the Lord would help her tell them about the Savior. They just might listen... maybe.

She felt bolder than ever as she thought of Robert and how he had witnessed to her despite her scoffing. Surely she could be as bold with Dale and Eric as Robert had been. Saturday morning she would go to the hospital. *I want to take them each a Bible; I wonder where I could get Bibles. Ah... the Ewings, I'll ask them, surely they will know.*

She had missed Robert at dinner, but the conversation

had so consumed her that she had hardly thought of him. But she still found herself thinking about him – even with a little bit of romance mixed in. She felt safe when she was with him and he made her feel important at the same time. He respected her and treated her, not as a jolly good fellow, but as a woman – *as a matter of fact, he just might be more romantic than he thinks... don't I hope!*

* * * * *

As she stepped onto the front porch of the house she shared with her mother, she was deep in thought about what to say to Eric and Dale when she went to the hospital. The house was an older home with a wide porch that was the width of the house. On the porch were two wicker chairs and matching table. Years past she and her mother would sometimes sit there and visit.

She was distracted with digging the key out of her purse with her thoughts far away when someone jumped up from one of the chairs and said, "Booo!"

Terri nearly fainted from the scare and she turned to run before she saw it was Mike.

"You are horrible!" She was angry, really angry. "You nearly gave me a heart attack. What's the idea? What are you doing here?"

"Haven't seen you around babe, where ya' been? The gang is getting kinda' small."

"Last time I was there you insulted me. I'm never coming back. When you were cursing you were using the name of Jesus – I love Him! He has given me peace and joy like none of our parties ever did. We were only fooling ourselves. Sorry, Mike, I don't want that any more."

"Awww, come on, baby, I'm sorry if I insulted you.

Can we go inside and talk?"

"No, my mother isn't home. We can sit here. What more is there to talk about?"

"Well, I really like you – guess I never told ya' before. I want to get together with you," Mike said as he sat back down. Dressed all in black and that was why she didn't notice him at first. She made a mental note to be more aware of her surroundings.

Terri sat on the edge in the other chair, but was being very wary of his every movement she remembered her pepper spray and cautiously felt in her purse as they talked, "It's no way, Mike. I used to do a lot of things that I shouldn't have, but I never slept with anyone... if that is what you are meaning."

"How 'bout I start going to church? It could be the church of your choice. I could say whatever I need to, or pay whatever it takes. My old man is pretty well fixed."

"It doesn't work that way. Church isn't the issue, Jesus is! To reform with the intent to have a physical relationship is using Jesus as a tool just like when you curse. Jesus is now the center of my life. I learned that I can't have both; your world and His world. I chose the later."

"Well, $%&# *if that's it,* you're impossible!" Mike said as he stood to go. She suddenly remembered she had told him her mother was not home, so she quickly stood with her one hand in her purse. She did not trust him. "If ya' ever change yer mind, I'll probably be at The Stripes. All that religious stuff just doesn't cut it with me, babe."

"I hear ya', but have you thought about Wyatt and Dennis and Mary?" she paused to steady her voice "they could be in eternity without a Savior – and I think you will know where that is, because you speak about it in almost every breath..." she could not go on.

Mike stood still and bowed his head. Had she touched a soft spot? Then he toughened himself up and said, "Well, gotta go!"

<hr>

"Bye, Mike. Think about it," and she turned and went into the house.

She sat on her bed trembling with fright of what might have happened. She had never been so outspoken in all her life. She felt sorry for Mike, but had no attraction to him at all.

———————

Chapter 12

Saturday morning dawned cold and rainy, which did very little to lift her spirits as she thought about the hospital visit she was planning. It would have been much easier and nicer to just curl up in a chair and read a book, but she had made up her mind what she needed to do and she would carry through. Mrs. Ewing had told her where there was a Christian bookstore so she could buy a couple of Bibles, so that was the first stop on her travels. She kept wondering what the guys would say to her gift. It would be the last thing either of them would have expected from her. Maybe they would totally refuse it, yet being in such bad physical condition she was hoping they would have done some serious thinking, just like she hoped that Mike would do... the guys death hardly bothered Mike at all showing they were not close friends at all.

The hospital was a huge building and since she had never been there before she did not know where to enter. After walking for what seemed like miles she found the correct door and was given their room numbers. Dale was on the second floor and Eric was on the third, so she decided to start at the top – Eric's room.

What a sight she saw when she stepped into his room after lightly knocking on his open door – most of his head and both arms were covered by bandages. There was no way she could recognize him.

"Eric?" she asked tentatively.

A mumbled answer sounded like, "Yeah?"

"I am Terri Nash, remember me?"

"Oh yeah, hey!" he brightened up and she could understand him better now.

"I saw the story about the wreck in the paper and heard you were here so I just want to say, 'Hi'. It sure is too bad about the accident. You look pretty bandaged up."

"Well, I was the only one out of the car who could do anything and the car was beginning to burn and Wyatt and Dennis were trapped in the front seat. I tried everything to get them out until my hands and arms were so burned I couldn't do any more. I can still hear their screams. They were basically burned alive and I couldn't do anything. Laying here thinking about that is worse than my burns. Terri, it is worse than a nightmare. I think about it all the time. I hear their screams even when I sleep."

"Oh, horrors, that is far worse than I could imagine. Do the doctors say how long you will be here?"

"No, they say it could be many weeks yet. It's like being trapped in hell... this place."

"That's interesting because I brought you a little gift that will help you be sure you are never 'trapped in hell' as you say. Jesus Christ is the answer to that. He will save you and give you a new life, as He has me." Saying this she opened the bag she carried and took out one of the Bibles and showed it to him. "Of course, you might not be able to read it until your bandages are off, but it is wonderful reading."

"Are you kidding... a Bible? I haven't cracked one of them open in years. I used to have to go to Sunday school when I was a kid, and I promised myself never to touch one when I got older. Thanks for your thoughts, but it may be a while... if ever. I didn't know you were a Bible person."

"Hey, I was like you. A few months ago I didn't know what a Bible was – well, almost. Then I met this guy at work... no, it is not romance, I know what you are thinking... but he talked to me about it and I found salvation in Jesus Christ, and it has been just what I needed. Eric, my life has done a complete 180 degree turn around and I love it.

"I think Jesus would also help you with the guilt you feel about Wyatt and Dennis."

After a long pause he said, "I can't imagine it! I thought religion is for sissies and bigots... I can't imagine someone nice like you..." and his voice trailed off.

"Eric, this isn't about religion, it is about a relationship with a person – Jesus Christ. Jesus Christ went deliberately to die – crucified on a cross so that God could wash your sins away if you would believe. It's true, Eric." Then after a pause and he said no more, "Well, I had better be going. I'll pray for you."

"Can you come back again, Terri, I liked the visit? I don't get many visitors, my family are mostly blown away on alcohol and drugs so they hardly ever come?"

"Yes, I'll come when I can. I plan to go down and see Dale now."

"Hey! Thanks for comin'."

"Bye! See ya' later. Hope you heal up soon."

As she left his room she thought, *I wonder how many other people think about Jesus and the Bible just like Eric does.* She could see in Eric what she must have looked like to Robert. How she wished he had been with her because he could have said these things so much better, but *I did what I could.*

Soon Dale's open door was in front of her so she lightly knocked and entered. Another very sad sight lay before her. One leg hanging from some kind of pulley and in a temporary cast and his left arm was also in a cast. He looked a mess! When he saw her he started to take a breath to say something and pain grabbed him in his chest because of broken ribs.

"Hi, Dale." Terri said as she walked up to the foot of his bed, "I'm sorry to see you like this. Are you in a lot of pain?"

"Terri, you're the last person I would have expected! These $%&# nurses won't give me pain meds when I need them. My breathing is the worst. I have to remember to take small short breaths. This whole $%&# mess has me just about to go out of my mind. I can't remember how I got into this $%&# mess anyhow. Suddenly I woke up in this bed. I think I was drunk and then all of a sudden this whole blur and a crash and laying outside on the freezing ground, but here I am. I can't get out of this place soon enough… they won't even give me one $%&# tiny drink."

"Dale, you got yourself into this. You always drank too much when we were out. You know life does not have to be like this, you can do something about it. I did! I have a whole new life and it's wonderful. I will never run around the way the bunch of us used to – never again.

"I brought you a little gift," she said as she reached into her bag, "that I hope you will look at and think about."

"A Bible!!" he took it in his right hand, "What kind of a $%&# nut do you think I am?" He spoke more loudly than he needed to.

"If you read it you will find something that will change

your life completely. In there it tells about a Man that died so that you won't have to go to hell."

"Ha! You forgot I'm a Jew?"

"It makes no difference whether you are a Jew or an Eskimo. Jesus Christ died so that all who believe on Him will not go..." He interrupted her.

"Now you've crossed the line – Jews believe that Jesus was just a good man like all the rest. We don't believe all that Christian mumbo-jumbo. We don't even believe there is a hell, except this room. Don't waste your time, Terri."

"I'm not wasting my time, because I have all eternity! Maybe Jews don't believe in Jesus," she had not thought of that before, "but neither do Muslims, nor Hindus, nor aborigines and a whole lot of others, but what we are talking about is that *you* need a Savior. You need peace, and satisfaction and a whole lot of other things. I put a marker in the Bible where I suggest you start reading.

"A few months ago I felt quite like you, but something happened in me as I read about how Jesus was crucified (by Jews, no less) and I realized that He went that way for me. I can tell you, Dale, the feeling of peace and joy in my heart is absolutely wonderful. Read it for me, one of your old buddies."

"All I can do is lay here in this $%&# bed staring at the TV. The last thing I need to do is read your book. Don't get your hopes up, girlie, I'm too Jewish to be fooled by Christian stuff, but maybe... for you I'll give it a shot sometime."

"OK, Dale, I gotta' go now. I'll pray for you and I'll try to come back."

"I would like you to come back – please do, just don't bring any more Bibles!"

"Bye, and I hope you get healed up soon."

Terri's brain was spinning as she left. *Here it is still before lunch and I feel more exhausted than after a whole day at work. I guess I was hanging around with a pretty bad crowd. My goodness, neither one of them was prepared to listen. I just hope they will read even just a little in the Bible at some point in time.*

When she arrived at her car she just sat there for a long time re-playing the visits with both guys. Neither one of them had ever been of interest to her romantically. And neither of them showed any interest in the Bible, so she decided to pray for them. Dale drank far too much, always! Eric was the group clown, and she and the other girls just giggled at his jokes – most of them dirty. Most evenings had started out with some wild dancing, but when the drinks had been flowing for a while most of them could not get their feet to do what they wanted; it was then that they headed to the cars for some car tag or just general chasing. She could see now the evenings had been as empty as they were full of noise and drinks.

* * * * *

When Terri arrived at the small meeting room that Sunday morning several of the people she had met before were already there. The Lambert family who had four children were already there, Mr. and Mrs. Rodgers, and Grace and Ella Taylor, older unmarried women. Terri sat in the same chair that she had set in on Monday and also on Thursday when she sat with Mrs. Ewing. No one spoke and she assumed this meeting, as Robert had said, is a very precious time beginning with remembering the Lord Jesus. Mr. Ewing had told her that she could not immediately participate in this meeting, but that they were hoping she would eventually want to.

She had read 1 Corinthians 11 again that morning to refresh her mind about what Mrs. Ewing had called "The Lord's Supper". As she looked at the small table in the center of the room it began to connect with the Scripture she had read. The bread was to remind us of the body of Jesus and the cup to remind us of the shed blood of Jesus and then she remembered Robert saying, "These things are only symbols to help us focus on the Person of Jesus and His love." She closed her eyes and prayed that the Lord would help her to understand. After a few moments she opened her eyes and the room was filling with the others and just then Mrs. Ewing arrived and sat next to her with a warm smile and a pat on the arm.

During the meeting they sang many hymns and all the men stood one by one and spoke in praise and worship. Terri was once again filled with a joy she had never known in all her 24 years – she could not help but smile. She had noticed that Robert was missing. After the meeting his mother said he decided to stay in New York and visit the ones that they fellowship with there. "He will be home late afternoon and asked me to tell you that he would like to take you to dinner this evening."

"Oh, that would be fine. I am so happy after this meeting I could stand up and clap!"

"I am really glad you enjoyed it, dear."

Just then Mrs. Lambert approached her and asked if she would like to join them at home for brunch. Another new experience for her – being invited to someone's home whom she hardly knew.

"I will be delighted to come. Shall I follow you?"

"What if I send James with you, he is 12 but knows his way around very well."

"Excellent!"

The Lambert home was nothing fancy to be sure; it was a much-lived-in family home. Mr. Lambert's occupation was remodeling homes and he did not make a lot of money, but they had everything they needed, and the children were calm and happy. She enjoyed visiting with them and Mrs. Lambert ("call me Jean" she had said) was very friendly and encouraging to Terri. She spent some time talking to each of the children. James was especially grown up in his talk and actions. She had enjoyed talking with him in the car and again at home. He told her he liked building model cars and beside his school work that seemed to be what he did most of the time. The younger ones each had to show her some treasure; sort of a show-and-tell. Then she sat and talked with Jerry and Jean for a while after brunch and soon it was time to return to the meeting room for the afternoon Bible reading and the Gospel.

Terri could hardly imagine all that she was learning. She realized she was just soaking it up. However, after the Gospel she suddenly remembered Robert wanted to take her to dinner... *wow! What an ending to a wonderful day,* she thought.

———

Chapter 13

Shortly after arriving home from the gospel preaching she received a phone call from Robert.

"Hi, Terri!" it was his now familiar voice, "how did it go today? Did you have a good time?"

"A good time? No, it was a <u>wonderful</u> time! The spirit of it was very special. How was your trip?"

"Oh, it was work, mostly work. However, the visit to the meeting in New York was very good. They are a group of very sincere brethren and there is a lot of love there. They are mostly black brethren."

"Black? Wow, I never pictured that, very interesting."

"The Black brethren are very real and very animated – you know, 'Hallelujah' and all that. Are you OK with having dinner with me? It won't be at such a fancy place as before. I'm thinking about the St. Louis Bread Company restaurant. What do you think?"

"Any place is fine with me." She said as she did a little *"Yes!!"* dance.

"I'll pick you up at 5:30, OK?"

"OK, I'll throw some ratty jeans on and a tank top and be ready! Bye." She was teasing so Robert just laughed.

Robert had heard from his mother about how Terri got along and that she had been invited to the Lambert's and it sounded like she was really fitting in and wanting to fit in. His father had preached and his text was, *"For the preaching of the cross is to them that perish foolishness; but unto us which are saved it is the power of God,"* and it was an excellent preaching, and Terri was very affected by it.

Besides her attending the meetings, and all, Robert was discovering that Terri was more and more on his mind. He had never dreamed the Lord would point him to someone like Terri and her not even a believer – *at first anyway! Well, we have become very good friends and I have resisted the urge to fall in love, but maybe I should give in. It seems the Lord has shown me the way.*

After the phone conversation with Terri, Robert was beginning to think seriously about courting her. In one sense he realized he hardly knew her, and yet he had been through the whole experience of her salvation and that had been a very precious experience, and built memories for both of them. However, he said over and over in his mind, *This is not a date... or is it, I just want to follow-up with her and see how she got along at the meetings. I've got to be strong for her, because I know how much the old life keeps tugging at me and it must be the same with her too.*

A short time later he was at her door ringing the bell. But when the door opened it was not Terri, but a young looking middle-aged woman, "Hello!" she growled in a husky smokers voice.

"Uh... hello! I'm Robert Ewing, is Terri home?" He stammered out.

"Yes, she is. I'm her mother. Good to meet you... would you come in... and I'll get her."

As he stepped into the room the TV was blaring away. He had never been in the house before so he noticed it was very neat and the furnishings were tastefully selected. He noticed a man on the sofa in front of the TV dressed in holey cut-off jeans and a 'T' shirt with a large picture of Marilyn Monroe on the front – obviously very much at home and quite a bit over-weight... too much at home. He looked over at Robert and nodded and mumbled something like, "Hi!" So Robert responded in kind and continued to take in the surroundings. Presently, Terri came bounding down the stairs dressed very nicely in a longer dress than he had seen before – *very beautiful, indeed!*

"Good evening, you look lovely tonight." He exclaimed.

"Thanks," then turning she called to her mother that she was leaving.

"OK, don't be late." Came from the kitchen. Robert thought is was peculiar coming from a woman who is seldom home.

As Robert began to drive, Terri slammed her hands into her lap and declared, "I don't understand that woman, she is supposed to be my mother. She is impossible! When I arrived home from the gospel meeting she said, 'where have you been all day?' I have not seen her in almost a month and then she asked that! I wanted to hit the ceiling, but in the calmest voice I have I said, 'To a gospel preaching'. Then she exploded." Terri was certainly upset.

"I'm so sorry! There is an old church song that says, 'God hath not promised sun without rain, Joy without sorrow, peace without pain.' Now I want to hear about your day. But first let's go in the restaurant and get situated."

After ordering and picking up their order they were able to get a booth where they could talk. The crowd at the restaurant was light, which kept the noise level down.

"Now, let's hear it from the start," Robert led off.

Then Terri described her feelings about each part of the Lord's Supper as best she could. How she remembered to link it with the Scriptures, and enjoyed the singing and noticed the beautiful words of the hymns. Then her visit with the Lambert's and the excellent time of speaking over the meaning of what had happened in the meeting earlier. She told about her time with the children and how she really loved children. She told about the Bible reading and the chapter suggested was Acts 8 and how Philip helped the traveler from Ethiopia to salvation in Jesus. Then she really enjoyed the gospel that Robert's father preached.

"All in all it was a wonderful day, until I met my mother and that *lump* she brought home. I told my mother about how I had taken Jesus Christ for my Savior, and the lump on the sofa said, 'Great!' His tone was mocking. Of course, my mother was worse when she asked me if I had gone soft in the head!

"Rob, Friday night was horrible. I was scared to death! I just don't trust the guys I used to hang out with any more. I came home after dark and walked up on the porch and was digging for my key when this guy jumps up off one of the chairs and hollers. It scared me so much that I spun around and nearly jumped down the stairs, and then I saw it was Mike." When Robert raised his eyebrows she said, "Yeah, the guy who insulted me at the bar. My knees were shaking, but I think I managed to control my voice. You can guess what he wanted... but what he got was the gospel. Well, I remembered you telling me that the name of God is a strong tower so that is what I used – the name of Jesus. He then asked if he started going to church if we could have a relationship. Boy, was I relieved when he left.

"Saturday wasn't much better. I went to the hospital and visited the two guys that were in the accident. I even took them each a Bible! Do you know what their response was?"

"No."

"The same as mine was when I caught you reading the Bible – I saw myself exactly." Then she giggled a little. "Yep, it was me exactly!"

"I am so proud of you I don't know how to say it. You were very brave."

"Well, I just did the best I could. I was wishing you were along because you would have been able to say it much better. At least Eric kinda' listened, but Dale said he was a Jew and his response was horrible. I sat in the car afterwards for a long time and had to cry, but then I prayed for them.

"However, today was a wonderful and new experience which I thoroughly enjoyed," she enthused.

"In the Bible reading this afternoon, did they speak about baptism?"

"Yeah, I wanted to ask about that this evening, but you keep asking questions!" Then she laughed, "I noticed how the traveler said, 'here is water, what hinders me being baptized.' Does that suggest that every believer should be baptized? How? And why?"

"Yes, it does," he said, "it's like becoming a citizen of a country. A person shows by baptism that he now belongs to Jesus."

"Well, if that is true I want to be baptized as soon as possible. I truly belong to another 'country'. Evidently the traveler was baptized in a pond but it's too cold now to use a pond." And she laughed.

"I had never thought of how we could do it! We normally baptize babies in the bathtub, but you are no baby! Let me talk to dad and mom and see what can be worked out."

Then he asked to hear more about of her hospital visit, and she, too, was intrigued with his work in New York and visit with the brethren there. It seemed like they had been apart for weeks and had a lot of catching up to do.

Then Robert mentioned a trip he and his parents were planning in three weeks time to Hamilton, Ontario. "There are special meetings over the weekend at the end of the month in Hamilton and I'm wondering if you would like to go with us. We will be driving. We will stay in a hotel while there. I'll see that all your expenses will be paid so there is no worry about that, and I'd really like for you to come along.

"There will be three meetings each day; Friday, Saturday and Sunday, and we will return after the gospel on Sunday. Those who live in Hamilton pay for the meals and hotel rooms, and I will see that your breakfast is taken care of. It will be a wonderful experience for you to meet others from around the world. It would really make the weekend complete for me too. What do you say?"

"Oh... uh... Oh my! I'm stunned, Rob," and she fidgeted with her napkin while she thought, then said, "Well, yes, being with you would be fun but the rest is quite scary. We once flew to California when I was young, as I told you, to see my grandparents, and otherwise I have never been so far from here. But will I fit in? Won't everybody be looking at me? If I could just hide in some corner I would be OK!" She was delighted and scared all at once.

"You would fit in just fine. That gorgeous dress

you have on is perfect. With the hat you bought you certainly will not stand out as a spectacle. My mother will stick close to your side and introduce you around. I will do all I can as well.

"There will be" he went on, "many other young women there too and you may find a kindred spirit."

"OK, I'll go! This is just too much all of a sudden. You are so kind and supportive – thank you. If I were back at my first life I would give you a kiss!" She exclaimed.

"Well, I guess a kiss wouldn't be so bad." He got up and gave her a quick peck on the cheek.

So the evening went by fast. Robert felt that it was so important for her to get her relationship with the Lord Jesus established before they think about their own relationship, but they both realized they were drawing closer together, *and so do my parents*, he thought. *Well, Lord, I'm beginning to see Your hand in all this but I'm still seeking You to guide me.*

* * * * *

"Could she dress in a sweat suit or slacks and blouse and get into the bathtub. She only needs to get her head under the water as far as I can see," said his father when Robert broached the subject of Terri's baptism.

"Would you baptize her, father?"

"Well, someone has to do it and yes, I would be honored."

The next day when Terri and Robert met at lunch he told her what his father had said.

"I do have a light weight running suit that I could wear and I guess if the tub was filled full enough of water I could dip my head under. I think I will feel kinda' foolish, but if that is what it takes I'll do it. I was thinking of that man who dipped seven times in the river, I think he felt foolish at first." She was a brave girl.

"Some of the other brethren will surely come, especially the Lamberts, and probably Ron and Alyssa also and we will have a short reading meeting to remind all of us of the importance of baptism. It will be in my parent's family room afterward. Jerry and Ron want to make it a lesson for their children so it will do two things. Perhaps Friday night would work – do you think?"

"Sure! Same time as the meetings, 7:30?" She rather nervously suggested.

"I'll try to arrange that, and I will pick you up and take you home. You shouldn't have to drive."

"Nah! I'll be fine, but on the other hand... I always enjoy it when you pick me up, of course."

So the baptism was set for that Friday and all the brethren were notified and invited.

———————

Chapter 14

Friday came all too soon, and yet in one sense not soon enough, and Terri was really apprehensive about the whole thing. On the one hand she felt like she was declaring her allegiance to her Lord, but on the other hand she felt like she would be a spectacle to all the folks attending. At lunch she shared her feelings with Robert and ask his suggestions.

"Robert, I am a bit scared about what is going to happen. I hate to be such a spectacle and yet I absolutely want to do this."

"I know how you must feel, but it must not be done in secret. John baptized Jesus in the Jordan River. In cffcct Jesus said it must be done publicly. Also, think about the children, by doing this you will demonstrate baptism for them, because they will not remember being baptized. The point for them as they grow up will be to learn what baptism means, and they certainly will remember your baptism. It is a wonderful opportunity, Terri, just calm your nerves."

"OK, I'll try. You have done such a good job explaining it to me I am really looking forward to it. Like salvation, this is another step in my spiritual journey. I'll see you tonight at 7 o'clock. I had better get back to my work now. Bye!"

"Bye! See ya' then."

When Robert pulled up to her house she came bounding out and didn't even wait for him to get out of the car. She was dressed in her running suit and had a small overnight bag in her hand – she was going through with this. She jumped into the car, a bundle of energy.

"Well, here I am in my running suit. You know, I have not been running for over a year. My mom and the lump, who looked up momentarily, wondered where I was going and I told them 'out'. I did not want an argument right now.

"This guy of hers is a total waste of space. I have never seen him do anything but watch TV. When mom talks to him he hardly listens. Oh well, I've got to get him out of my mind for now. Is everything ready at your house?"

"Yes, I think it was just about when I left. No one had arrived yet, but it was too early." Just seeing how she handled the emotional aspect of her committal to the Lord and now baptism was causing love to flood into his heart.

When they got to his house a few others had arrived so Terri quickly went into the spare bedroom because she felt self-conscious. A few minutes later Mrs. Ewing came in and said the water was warm and ready and took her hand as they went into the bathroom where Mr. Ewing was waiting. She stepped out of her sandals and into the tub and sat down. The water was nice and warm but very wet! Then everyone quieted and she noticed a few of the children crowding in behind Mr. Ewing each trying to see. He was smiling a reassuring smile at her. After a few moments he laid his hand on her shoulder and began to speak, "I now baptize you Terri Rachel Nash to the Name of the Father and of the Son and of the Holy Spirit, in the name of the Lord Jesus Christ, Amen."

At that moment he indicated she bend forward, which she did submerging nearly her whole head under the

118

water and back up. Her hair was over her face and dripping wet and he whispered, "Very good!" So she stood as Mrs. Ewing handed her a large bath towel and she wiped her face brushing her hair out of her eyes. They told the children, who stood with their mouths and eyes wide open, to go back to the family room, and she went back into the spare bedroom to dry off and change.

That wasn't bad at all! I can't believe that it is all over. Thank you Lord Jesus for all you brought me into with this family and these friends, she prayed silently as she dressed. The house was quiet except for the children's loud whispers, some of them wondering what happened to Terri. They were assured she was all right and would be out soon. The children seemed relieved when she appeared dressed for meeting, hat and all, even though her hair was pretty damp.

They all sat around in the family room and had a Bible reading. Mr. Ewing suggested some Scriptures specifically about baptism, so she listened very closely not wanting to miss anything that was said. Afterward, refreshments were served. Some of the children came over to stand in front of her and just look. Of course, the Lambert children knew her so they asked all sorts of questions.

"Did you get water in your nose?" one squeaky voice asked.

"Was it scary under the water," another childish question.

"Did you have your eyes open?"

"I can go under the water when I swim!"

She had to laugh at some of the ways children think. She hugged as many of them as she could, but soon Robert indicated he could take her home if she wished. Well, she *was* rather worn out.

When they arrived at her house the lights were all out meaning her mother had gone to bed for which she was glad – she did not want questioning. Robert walked her to the door and this time he took her shoulders and turned her to face him and said, "You were absolutely wonderful tonight. The whole thing went perfectly and everyone seemed so pleased, and the children were stunned about the whole thing. They will not forget this for a long time." He then pulled her close and kissed her with a proper kiss. "Goodnight, see you at work."

She savored the moment by leaning into him, not wanting this to stop. For her everything was in slow motion, but still it was too short. He finally moved back obviously enjoying it himself. He whispered, "Well, I better go. You are so sweet." As he turned toward the car she managed a whispered "Bye! Love ya!"

* * * * *

She went to her bedroom immediately. She was not hungry, she was just exhausted from the strain of it all, and she touched her lips – *he kissed me! He kissed me! I can't believe it. Oh, that felt so right!* She sat on the edge of her bed and played back that moment over and over. Then she began to think of the whole evening. She felt so good about it. She was thrilled that she could do something that Jesus would appreciate. She was done with her old life – drinking, dancing, hanging out and all the other rowdy things she used to do – forever gone!

Then suddenly a feeling of being so crude... the way she spoke and acted brought awful questions into her mind. These people, including Robert, seemed so polished or something... she wondered if she could ever really fit in. *Will I at some point find I can't live this way? Will I disappoint everybody, even Jesus? Oh Lord, I don't want to be a disappointment!* So she got down on her knees at the side of her bed and covered her head with the tissue she held and began to pour out her heart to the Lord Jesus. *Lord Jesus, take this uncertainty away. Change me so I will fit in with Your people. I have these moments, Lord, when I am not sure... I need Your help.* She told Him she wanted to be here for Him whatever it took. She would do whatever He wanted. She told Him she loved Him for bringing her to this moment. Her heart was full of the Lord Jesus as she said *"Amen."*

Before getting undressed and into her pajamas she locked her door. She was never sure whether the Lump was there or not and she sure did not trust him. Sometimes he would just leer at her as she went about the house. She remembered just then that she did not remember his name and she was sure her mother had said it; maybe Dirk or Dork... Oh well, it did not matter.

Tomorrow was Saturday and Robert had said his mother wanted her to come for supper. What Edith actually had said was, "I just cannot bear to think of Terri eating alone or maybe even with her mother and friend, why don't you invite her for dinner tomorrow?" So, for Terri, that was something to look forward to. She was beginning to feel at home with the Ewing's and enjoyed visiting with them. She found out that Robert's father had worked for Kodak all his life as a film research scientist. His stories were interesting. She got to see another side of the company, which was fun. And when Robert and his dad started talking "shop" she could see that Robert had an advantage in making the displays because he knew some of the history.

As they sat visiting after supper, Robert asked, "Have you ever played ping-pong?"

"Umm... I've played it little. I never got good."

"Well, how about a game. We've got a table in the basement."

"Sure! I promise I won't cry when I get beaten." She chuckled.

As it turned out, she was a master of the understatement "...I won't cry..." Robert remembered those words after about 5 matches and he had lost them all!!

"Umm... maybe we should do something else," he appeared sad yet he laughed, "I'm about to cry! I'm glad you *never got good* at the game!" and they both laughed together. "What other things did you 'never get good at'?" They were now both laughing so hard that it took her a few seconds to answer.

"Oh, Monopoly and Scrabble and games like that."

There was a sofa and easy chairs in the basement family room so they sat on the sofa and talked and talked for quite a while, and then shortly after they finished the ping-pong Rob said, "Let's go for a drive and get some ice cream."

So they hopped into his car and drove to the University campus and he showed her where he went to school and as they drove she pointed to several bars and nightclubs that had been her "previous life." They drove by the place where the accident happened that killed Wyatt and the others.

"I think I'll go back and visit those guys in the hospital sometime... they are going to be in there for a while if my guess is right. Maybe they'll be ready to talk. What do you think?"

"Sure! As someone has said, 'just give them Jesus'." Just so long as you don't go falling in love with one of them!" He said with a broad smile.

"Oh, don't you worry! Not in a thousand years." She emphasized each word.

"Here's an ice cream place, how about stopping here?"

"Umm... I'd prefer not just now. The old gang came here a lot... not a good place."

"No problem, I didn't know, never been there." He was glad she spoke up." There's Charly's Ice Cream Shoppe about a mile ahead. That would be fine for me."

"Hey, ice cream is my one weakness!" Anywhere would have been fine, just to be with him.

Later that evening they returned to his house since she had left her car there. She had had a wonderful evening. They had talked about a lot of things – just everyday stuff. Before this they had talked so much of the Lord's things they had not got down to everyday living. There was no kiss at the end of the rainbow this evening and she did not want to push him for one. *Maybe last night he was just carried away by the baptism and all.*

Now tomorrow was Sunday – *or rather the Lord's Day* – and she was looking forward to the meetings. The folks at the meeting were getting friendlier all the time, but she had a sense that several of them were a little worried that she was trying to "catch" Robert. *Am I?* She asked herself. *Absolutely not! I've come to know Jesus and am learning more about Him every day and that has nothing to do with Rob, except that he helped me through all this. Of course, Rob is very nice as well as knowledgeable about God's things, but I'm sincere with myself when I say Jesus has been my focus.*

The next day the meetings went very well for her. The gospel was very appealing and took her back to the moment when she first realized she needed a Savior. She loved to rethink that whole experience. Then Ronald Rogers asked her to come for dinner that night. She was looking forward to visit with them.

"I wanted to ask you, Terri," Ronald asked after dinner and little Peter had been put to bed, "what ever happened to everybody after I left?"

"Most of the kids were still there doing the same things after you left, but, of course, you would have heard about the accident."

"Accident? No?"

"On the 2nd of this month five of the my gang had a car accident and 3 were killed and 2 were badly injured. Wyatt and Dennis were burned to death in the front seat and Mary was thrown from the back seat through the front windshield. Dale was badly burned trying to rescue Wyatt and Dennis and Eric was thrown out with badly mangled legs. Eric and Dale are still in the hospital as far as I know. They were all so drunk or high that neither of the boys knew why they were in the hospital. I visited them a couple of weeks ago and gave them both a Bible, which neither of them wanted. Dale was the most difficult because of his background." She paused to get a breath.

"No, I had not heard. It really makes you think. I suppose it could have been you or I. For me I finally began to see where that kind of life was leading. I know I caused my folks an awful amount of heartache. Somehow I just made bad friends and followed along.

Oh, sorry, I didn't mean that you were bad!"

"Oh, I was, Ron. I made fun of Rob when I saw him reading his Bible and told him it was just fairy tales. The trouble was I thought he was really handsome and he was always so calm, seemed so stable. As we talked at lunch he gradually helped me to understand the Bible. But, just like you, I began to realize that the course I was on was empty. Of course, I didn't have the Christian home background like you did.

"Rob has helped me to see that even a tiny sin is sin. I had a terrible flashback the other day when I remembered when you and I were so drunk that I vomited all over you!" Alyssa gasped! "What a horrible life that was." Terri paused as they laughed. "I am sorry, Alyssa, to go on like this but Ron and I were certainly friends, but it never was more than that. We were not in love, at least, from my side and in the world friends do things like that."

"Nor from mine either," Ronald put in, "although I thought you were pretty nice I will have to admit."

"Now, instead of being just friends we are brother and sister in the Lord. I truly love my new family, and want to be here for the Lord Jesus as best I can. I have found such peace in my heart."

So it was a quiet evening with many excellent discussions on the Lord's things... things Terri and Ronald were now both enjoying.

———————

Chapter 15

Monday morning came soon enough after all the excitement over the baptism, and the meetings on Sunday, and then visiting with Ron and his Alyssa. Terri was struggling to remember everything she was learning but she was enjoying her new life. She and Robert found they were meeting at lunch more often recently because they had now become company for each other and enjoyed visiting. This Monday she had a question, or rather a conundrum, to ask Robert, and he had something to tell her.

"Rob, I have a problem and please don't take what I say the wrong way, because I don't know how to ask it. I think you know I enjoy everything wonderful well; your parents have been angels, the other brethren too, and above all the meetings, but this one thing keeps nagging at me. I read 1 Corinthians 11 as you suggested, but I guess I don't understand it enough. I was always taught that women are equal to men and that we women must push forward to accomplish it. Even in the house or restaurant it is always the man that gives thanks for the food," she looked into his eyes sincerely.

"Well... um..." he was pausing to think of how best to answer her, "I guess the answer is very simple. God has ordered it that way. I know you want more than that, but it is God's ordering and we choose to live with that as our standard.

"God created Adam first," he went on, "and put him in charge of naming the animals and caring for the Garden of Eden. Then God saw that Adam needed a

126

helpmate and God created Eve out of Adam's side, but she was not his equal in the sense that He had given Adam certain things to do, Eve was a helpmate. Then she fell prey to Satan's suggestion and convinced Adam to eat of the Tree and he did. This brought sin into the world, but God held Adam responsible although Eve had to suffer the consequences in her own way – pain in childbirth. Adam should have been the head. Therefore, while we are on this earth and subject to sin and the penalty of death the woman is not equal to man as far as public function and domination. Paul says in 1 Corinthians 11, where you read, that man is head of the woman, Christ is man's head, and God is Christ's head. This Scripture does not mean just men and women who are Christians, but the principle applies to all men and women, yet it is violated on every hand in the world and even in some Christian circles, but *we* choose to try to live by it."

"I still don't think it is fair, although what you say makes perfect sense. I think some women are more capable than some men. Some cultures make women just a man's property, she has no say in anything. What about that?"

"Those cultures are mostly dominated by Satanic influences and yet they do it in the name of a religion, one that they invented. However, that is not God's way at all, nor is it the believing Christian's way. You are right; some women are more capable than men, but that does not change God's order. If men are to be responsible and bear the responsibility of every decision then they need good training as they grow up. What is needed is a capable mother – like the woman of worth in Proverbs – who is with God about her children and household, and a loving and understanding helper to her husband... do you see how important a strong household is?"

"That helps a lot, but I need to think about it. I was truly wondering not arguing, I really want to understand it, and you have helped." She gave him one of her smiles and stood to return to work, "I hate to end this but Judy will have my neck if I am late! See you at prayer meeting."

Robert was left with a whirlwind of thoughts and Scriptures in his mind. *Did I tell her the right thing? She has such a good and willing spirit.* He was actually very pleased she asked the question because it troubles many Christians and especially women. As he walked back to his office he mulled over this whole subject and determined to study on it and pray.

Oh, I forgot to tell her I'm going out of town again. I guess I'd better tell her after prayer meeting. Boy, I don't like all this traveling they have me doing, but I must admit I'm getting some good ideas. He mumbled to himself.

* * * * *

That evening Robert drove his parents to the meeting. It was a beautiful evening, a time of year he enjoyed. His mother was commenting on the various trees that had already begun to turn to their beautiful reds and yellows. Many of the flowers had already nodded their heads and given in to the approaching winter, but not the mums and colorful kale so many flowerbeds were still gorgeous. Robert's artistic mind was framing all the photos he could take of the flowers. His favorite hobby being photography – after all, he worked at a photography museum. One of the first things he had bought after he got his job was a good camera and extra equipment. He made a mental note that he wanted to get some photos of the season's flowers, *and, come to think of it I don't have a decent photo of Terri.* Then he said to himself, *I guess I had better make up my mind about this girl.*

By the time he had thought through all of this they had arrived at the prayer meeting. His mother had said something to him but he couldn't remember what it was. Terri came in shortly after they were seated and she sat in her usual place by his mother. As he watched he thought, *I am really proud of her.*

When the meeting closed Robert soon found himself at her side and he took hold of her arm and whispered, "How about I meet you at your place and we go get some ice cream?"

"You're going to get me as fat as a pig!" She said with a big smile, "Great, see you there."

Charly's it was again and since it was Monday night there were hardly any others beside themselves. It was a good place to talk and the ice cream was an added bonus.

"Look, I forgot to tell you at lunch..." and she interrupted him.

"Don't worry about it, Rob, I have not had any time to think about that subject anyway."

"No, it's not about that. I have to go away again."

"When?"

"I will leave on Wednesday for several days in Chicago at the Museum of Science and Industry. They are one of the most progressive museums in the world, and my boss thinks I could pick up some ideas. They have scheduled me to return home on Saturday, but I told them I would like to return on a flight Sunday afternoon. That way I could visit the brethren there. I hate all this traveling, but I guess it has been worth it."

"I hate to see you go away again, but I guess the Lord knew what He was doing for a couple of reasons; my salvation being the first, and then that you can visit other meetings like this."

"Well, you say that so nicely, but I might as well say what I am really thinking..." he nervously cleared his throat and swallowed the lump in it before continuing "I think the Lord put me in the museum where we work so I could meet you. I'm kind of a slow thinker, I guess, but I believe you are the one He wanted me to meet. I've tried to keep romance out of our relationship until I knew which direction you were headed. Now I'm sure of one thing and that is I would like to officially begin courting you, if you will have me?" His smile couldn't have been more complete and his cheeks cherry red.

Terri was stunned even though she had thought they were on a collision course with courtship, the sudden reality of it took her breath away. When she found her voice she said, "Well, I don't know Mr. Ewing I will need to think about that for a while..." in her most teasing voice as she looked down at her ice cream. And he waited with an expectant smile.

After barely 2 seconds she said, "OK, I've thought about it and the answer is YES!" and she fairly shouted it, and began laughing with tears streaming down her face.

The workers all looked over and supposing it was a marriage proposal they all began to clap, which embarrassed Terri, "I am so happy because I have been thinking the same way... when can we start? Can we start from about a month ago?" Then they both laughed. "In my first life I would have gotten up and danced; I am so happy."

Robert was really excited and shocked that he had

130

taken the step. "Well, I have a confession to make. When we first met back in July something happened inside of me that had never happened like that before, but I couldn't let it take over. I did not want to ever marry an unbeliever. In all soberness, I want to be sure that we act like Christians in our courtship. I have fallen in love with you – no question."

"I think it will be such a privilege to be courted by you and I think what you say is right. As I said, my world and my concept of these things was so different before I became a Christian." It was obvious she was delighted.

The restaurant staff all still wished them well after they heard it was not a marriage proposal. They walked to the car arm and arm, both of them beaming huge smiles.

On the ride home Terri said, "I have not written to my dad for years, do you think it would be OK for me to write him about *us*? I could ease in something about my conversion as well. I have no idea how he will take it."

"By all means, I would be delighted for him to know. He certainly must have also changed in all those years. Maybe he has become a believer himself. Sure go ahead, I like the idea."

So the next evening she wrote and rewrote a letter to her father. She had not heard from him in years so she assumed he lived at the address she had in her book. Would he get all steamed up like her mother when she told her about becoming a believer in Jesus Christ, or... *Well, I will find out soon enough if he even bothers to reply.*

* * * * *

"Good Morning, Mr. Nash," the maid said as she

walked into his penthouse apartment high above New York City, "I have your mail."

"Good Morning, Sally. Just lay it on the counter. I am just putting my shoes on. I'll be ready for breakfast momentarily."

"I'll do that and I'll put the coffee on. What would you like for breakfast?"

"Actually, coffee and cold cereal sounds best this morning. Thank you."

Kenneth Nash was CEO at Forward Electronics, Corporation, but instead of going to the office this morning he was expected to speak at the Chamber of Commerce of New York City monthly breakfast. It was a real "plum" to be asked to address such an elite group of businessmen.

He decided to scan what mail had arrived and he was dumbfounded to see an envelope addressed in a feminine handwriting. The postmark said Rochester, New York. *Who could this be from... certainly not from Muriel! She has not written in years – of course, neither have I. Oh no! Maybe something happened to Terri.* With this thought he fairly ripped the envelope open, forgetting the rest of the mail. It was a letter *from* Terri, he could not believe his eyes.

Dear Dad,

I have not heard from you in so long I wonder how you are. Do you live alone? I hope this gets to you as I used the only address I have.

Well, I recently got a job at the George Eastman House Museum working the admissions desk and I love it. I saved up and bought an old car so I can get to work. I wasted a lot of time running around after high school, which got me nowhere. It seemed like fun at the time, but now I realize it was a waste. I still live at home (the above address) and that works out OK.

The wonderful thing I wanted to tell you is that I have been saved by the blood of Jesus. He has made a fantastic change in my life and I have peace that I never knew before. I hope you won't think I have joined a cult or something.

I met Robert Ewing – he is the design director at the museum – and he helped me understand salvation through Christ. He is a wonderful friend – a year older than me. This is one reason I am writing – we have just begun to court and I would like you to meet him sometime. No we are not shacking up together. He lives with his parents. I think you will like them, his dad is a PhD in biochemistry and he worked designing film for the Kodak Company.

I would like to see you sometime if you ever come this way.

Your daughter,

Terri

Ken just sat back in his chair stunned, his sweet daughter thinking of marriage already. It seems like she was just a little girl. *My fault, I have never gone back. I was so angry at Muriel that I never wanted to see Rochester again. How awful! My little girl is the one who suffered. Well, I had better get this speaking engagement over with and do some deep thinking.* "Sally, will you get Jason to bring the car around to the front of the building?" He had to leave immediately to be on time.

* * * * *

For Robert the euphoria of the night before and decision to begin courting had to be set aside when work started because he had to prepare for his trip to Chicago. These trips, which were mainly for education, did not mean that any project he was working on could be delayed. So he had to work twice as hard. Most days he was eating his lunch in his office and sometimes working until late. Some days Terri would sneak in and eat with him, but even that was a distraction. His heart did flip-flops whenever she was around, but this time he had to exclude her since he was leaving so soon.

They had an evening together on Tuesday when Terri ate dinner with Robert and his parents and then the two of them went to the lower level and sat and talked until late. They had so much to talk about, joining their hopes and dreams. They each wanted to know about the childhood of the other, and where they went to grade school, and high school, and did they have lots of friends? When you are planning a life together you want to know everything about each other. Even though they were not together all those years the experiences of each other become virtual memories. Soon the evening had to end as Robert had an early flight to Chicago, and Terri had to go to work. Parting was getting even harder than before.

Chapter 16

He had enjoyed the trip and was amazed at the size of the museum. "I sure hope someday I can take you to see the museum," Robert enthused the first time he was with Terri after returning from Chicago, "it is fantastic! You could walk all day and never see all of it. The displays are very professional, especially the interactive ones. Boy, did I ever get some great ideas!"

"It sure sounds like you had a good time, I'm so glad." Terri appreciated hearing all about it. "Was it all in one building?"

"Absolutely, one huge building left over from the 1893 World's Fair. They said it was made of wood overlaid with plaster and was going to be demolished until some wealthy business men decided it should be saved and they spearheaded an effort to do that. Gradually over the years the exterior was replaced with stone. It is in many respects a beautiful building."

"That does sound interesting. I sure hope we can go see it sometime." Terri was thinking... *it would make a good honeymoon spot!* "Did you see the brethren there?"

"Yes, and believe it or not some were asking about you. They had heard about your conversion through Alyssa, of course, they did not know about *us* and I didn't enlighten them. Several said they were hoping to go to the meetings in Hamilton this weekend, so we'll probably see them there. That reminds me, we will be leaving Friday morning about 7:00. Hope you will be ready. The drive is about 3 hours and the first meeting is at 11:00. This is going to be so much fun having you along; it was always just dad and mom and me before." His anticipation was written all over his face.

"I am a little apprehensive about meeting so many new people, but I am excited about going with you and your folks. I have never taken a long road trip... never! Dad worked all the time and we didn't have anywhere to go. He and mom left me with a babysitter a couple of times and they went somewhere, but the last time I can remember was when I was maybe 7 and I hated the babysitter. She was fat and always hollering at one of her own kids or at me, so my idea of a vacation is not a good one at all. I am so looking forward to this! You know, I have never even been to Niagara Falls!"

"I can't believe it and you live so close. Some Saturday you and I will go there. Let's plan it for spring when it is warm enough to enjoy it. Have you ever been to Hershey, Pennsylvania where they make the candy?"

"No. As I said we never went anywhere except here."

"Well, we've got to go there I know you like chocolate. That is a sight to see – all the chocolate." He paused for a moment then asked, "How about Corning Glass Works? Oh well, I guess the answer is 'No'. That is where they make all kinds of glassware... it is very interesting. We've got to go to some of these places."

"You have so many good ideas. I think I'll like to travel with you and go to these places – together – won't that be fun?"

Whenever they had a night like this where they could sit and talk they loved sharing old memories and experiences with each other. The nights were never long enough, but since they were both working they had to make the most of each time together. Because they had to do their own laundry and ironing and be ready for the next day at work. Robert's mother had long since refused to do his laundry except in rare cases... *Part of cutting the apron strings* she had said. So consequently the two of them were not together as often during the week as they would have liked. The time after the meetings on Monday and Thursday were the best times for them during the week. Then Saturday they often spent together. However, this week they were traveling to Hamilton, Ontario for a Bible Conference on the weekend and Terri was excited about that.

* * * * *

As they drove up to the Nash's home Friday morning Robert jumped out and hurried to the front door in time to meet Terri coming out with a small case. She looked flustered and she told Robert as he took her case that her mother had just hollered at her for leaving for a whole weekend, and to study the Bible no less! Robert remembered the Scripture that says, *"Yea, and all that will live godly in Christ Jesus shall suffer persecution."* He felt so sorry for Terri having to suffer such words from her mother. Terri was quiet for a long while, which for her was quite unusual, but she was obviously praying. His father and mother in the back seat sensed that she was praying so they were quiet. After a while she commented at something along the road and they all knew she was OK.

Robert's father leaned forward to speak directly to her. "Do you think your mother believes in God?" His voice was soft.

"I don't really know, Mr. Ewing. I think she probably

believes there is a God, but she does not want him interfering in her life. I know, because I was like that not long ago." This conversation lasted almost half of the trip as Henry was interested in what she said about how she thought of God.

Terri wondered if they would go close enough to the Falls to see them, but Robert said they would be close but not that close. Mr. Ewing told them about a book he had read, which told about the various attempts by people to go over the falls in a barrel or other contraption. Some had died and some had lived. He also told about a time when he and Edith were first married and they went to the falls and, because of the mist from the water they saw an almost completely round rainbow. "It stopped at our feet, but there was no pot of gold!" They all had a laugh about that.

The weather had been bright and sunny for their drive, but the air had a frosty nip to it. Soon they were pulling into the parking lot at the school where the meetings were to be held. As Robert and his folks got out of the car; Terri took a deep breath and did the same, thinking, *Well, here goes!* There were quite a few young people standing around by the door as they walked up. Most of the young people greeted the Ewing's, but just stared at Terri as she walked with her hand in Robert's arm. The fact was she was squeezing his arm until it hurt. "Would you not squeeze so hard?" He whispered. "Oh, my goodness, I didn't realize!" she replied and relaxed her grip with a nervous giggle.

Inside there was just a sea of people standing around renewing old acquaintances and to Terri there was not a face she recognized. *O dear, what have I got myself into,* she thought. But Robert was very good and introduced her to as many as he could.

"Good morning, Mr. & Mrs. Cunningham, it's good to see you again. This is Terri Nash whom you were asking about last weekend." Then he turned to Terri and introduced them to her as Alyssa's parents.

"Good to meet you. I had dinner with Ronald and Alyssa a week ago. I think little Peter is adorable."

"Yes, we think he is too. We are so glad to make your acquaintance. If you can, we would be glad if you would visit us sometime." Mrs. Cunningham seemed very friendly.

"Thank you, I would like that." But now it was about time for the first meeting,

Some indicated that they had heard of her conversion and welcomed her quite warmly. She, meanwhile, was trying to remember names, but it was hopeless, but what nearly blew her mind was that she had met people from England, Scotland, Germany and Australia. *Once I get to know people, it is going to be fun.*

The newest experience for her was how the meetings were conducted. It seemed one man had been invited to suggest which Scriptures to read in each meeting and fielded the questions and comments. She tried her best to follow and did get quite a few good thoughts, but with her limited knowledge of Scripture it was difficult. Mrs. Ewing was good to help her find the various Scriptures referred to. The addresses, or were they sermons, each afternoon, and the gospel on Sunday afternoon were easier to follow.

She enjoyed talking to various ones and each day she took a walk with Robert to "stretch our legs". The hotel where everyone stayed was very nice and comfortable. Her room was on the same floor as Robert's room and that of his parents. They all went to breakfast together. But Sunday came all too soon and after the gospel they said their 'goodbyes' to those they knew and were soon on their way home. She had been on a 'high' all weekend but on the trip home she had a kind of let 'down' feeling. *Probably it's that I have been able to forget everything and now I have to face the situation at home once again.* But the conversation all the way home was about the weekend and what each one remembered and enjoyed. Terri had met several young people from overseas and had enjoyed some long and fun conversations; finding out what their home country was like and their families, and they wanted to hear about her former life in the "world" and then her conversion.

* * * * *

Winter this year in Rochester came in with a blast just after Thanksgiving. Some snow storms piled up a lot of snow, which made driving slow and hazardous. As it turned out Terri found that she was eating more meals with Robert's family than she was eating at home. Especially whenever she knew her mother would be home, which was more often since Dirk had moved in with her, or at least, it seemed that he had moved in as he was almost always watching TV. He was the most distasteful man she had ever met and she was praying that the relationship might not hurt her mother. She was also really afraid for her own safety when he was around. Each time she arrived home she would go immediately to her room and lock the door. Although, she felt relatively safe as long as her mother was there at the same time, her experience as a child had changed her for life.

She felt perfectly free to just drop in at the Ewing home at anytime, and they had told her to do that. There was always plenty of food prepared because his mother loved cooking. Whenever she had to go home after dark or even when there was a lot of snow on the ground Robert would follow her home and make sure she was safely inside. Some nights she phoned him from her room to assure him she was OK. Fortunately for Terri, Dirk was only seldom there without her mother.

When Christmas arrived the Ewing's planned a great Christmas feast and had invited all the local brethren in for a dinner and Mrs. Ewing asked Terri to help her, so Terri was flattered and arrived at the house mid-morning. The food was to be set out cafeteria style in the kitchen. With twenty-three mouths to feed it took a lot of food and there was not table space for a formal dinner, so the adults had lap trays while the small children sat around the table and their parents prepared their plates. After Mr. Ewing gave thanks for the food and the food-line began it was Terri's responsibility to see that everyone had a drink. There was ice water and several types of pop as well as iced tea. There was a special treat for the children – chocolate milk. When everyone was nearly done she served coffee and hot tea to those who wished it, and assisted Robert in passing around dishes of the goose and turkey and vegetables to those who would like seconds.

None of them missed having a Christmas tree or other Christmas decorations except Terri. Everywhere she saw people decorating for Christmas but not the Ewing's so she made a mental note of it to ask Robert. However, at the Ewing's the mood was certainly festive and there was a continual hum of voices. Some sat in the lower level and some in the living room as it was not possible for everyone to fit in one room.

When the meal was over Mr. Ewing asked Robert to play the piano and they all sang together a number of hymns. Terri did not know that Robert could play so beautifully, but she was very proud of him. They sang hymns such as, "Christ is the Savior of sinners," and "We'll sing of the Shepherd that died," and "I will sing of my Redeemer," and many more. Actually they sang until they could not sing any more and the little children were getting restless and needed their beds. When the party was over Robert and Terri went downstairs to sit and relax, and the elder Ewing's went to bed. Mrs. Ewing was totally exhausted. She had been at work since early morning, because she had to put the turkey and goose into the oven very early.

———————

Chapter 17

Soon the holidays were fading into memory and winter was upon them in earnest with lots of snow and cold. Buffalo, New York, which is close by is known for huge lake-effect snows. The people in the whole area are used to lots of snow, but it still slows traffic down and makes it difficult getting from place to place. And whatever snow shoveling got done at her house had to be done by Terri as Dirk was too busy watching TV! *Grrrrr!* The cars had to be off the street so the snow plows could get through, so this made it mandatory that she shovel. Several times when the snowfall was extra heavy Robert came over and helped her. Her mother could not complain because many times Terri shoveled so her mother could get her car out too. She hoped her mother would get the hint that the guy she had chosen was a loser.

Robert and Terri tried to plan to have Saturday evenings together whenever possible. Several times they went out for dinner to a Mexican or Chinese restaurant and then returned to his house to visit.

One evening when he arrived to pick up Terri for dinner, he was pleased to see Terri's mother's car was not there, but when Terri met him at the door she looked upset and she just waved him in. There was her mother all crumpled up on the sofa and crying her eyes out so he gave Terri a questioning look and she whispered, "Dirk took her car and left and said he was not coming back – ever."

"Did she call the police?" he asked. "Surely they can send out an alert."

"No," Terri said, "mom had just signed him onto the vehicle title so they both owned it together."

Robert's response was a look of horror, and he shrugged and threw up his hands. "Nothing can be done, she basically gave him the car. What about the house did she do that also?"

"I don't think so."

"No," her mother said through her sobs, "I wouldn't be that dumb!"

"Well, there is nothing any of us can do about the car. We'll just have to help you get to work or wherever you need to go." Robert said to Muriel as he motioned to Terri that they should be going since there was nothing they could do for her mother at the moment.

It was pizza this time and as they arrived at the restaurant he mused, "I think they had a spat and Dirk will return soon. Just my guess!"

"Yeah, her tears were probably not so much about the car."

Then Terri jumped a little and grabbed her purse, "I almost forgot... I've got a letter from my dad." She produced an envelope and quickly opened it and began reading.

> Dear Terri,
>
> Life for me has been very hectic these last few years I keep forgetting to write or call you. I suppose you have grown into a beautiful young woman. Someday I hope to fly to Rochester to see you. I am glad you have found a young man, Robert Ewing, to love and who loves you. If he is everything you say he must be a very special person. I hope you will have a long life together.

Sometimes I miss your mother, but I am sorry how it all worked out.

Your grandparents in California have both died in the last few years. I have inherited their estate since I am the only living child. The mansion sold for several million dollars. Selling that has added to my normal workload plus travels to the four-winds. No, I do not have a girlfriend – I think that is what your question meant.

As far as Christianity, I will admit to having some serious thoughts about the hereafter, but have never taken any time to think it through. If I come I would like you and Robert to talk to me about it.

I assume you two will be married soon – just from the way you talk – please send me an invitation, I will come if I can.

You were always the joy of my life and I am so sorry for not seeing you grow up. Please give my regards to Muriel, but don't get her hopes up.

Your affectionate father.

They both sat in stunned silence at what Terri had just read. It was much better than she had expected – much better! He was even open to hear the gospel! What had she said in her letter; she could not remember? It must have been the right thing, but it was several weeks ago. She had tears in her eyes when she turned to Robert and said, "I cannot believe it! I just can't! All these years and no contact! Of course, I could not afford to go to New York but I should have written him or called him."

"True, but he could have done the same, in fact, with his money he could have come to see you but he didn't. Oh well, at any rate that is a very good letter – very kind of him."

* * * * *

The following Monday Robert's phone rang at his desk and he caught it, as usual, on the first ring.

"Robert Ewing, Displays."

"Robert!" His mother fairly shouted into the phone, "Come quick, your dad is terribly sick."

"I'll be right there, mom. Should I call the ambulance?"

"Yes, do. He is really bad!"

So after alerting his boss to the situation he ran to the car and was home very soon. The ambulance had not arrived yet, but his father was lying on the sofa moaning. His mother whispered to him what happened, so when the paramedics arrived he was able to tell them. He elected to drive with his mother following the ambulance as closely as possible. His mother thought it was a stroke, but she was so distraught that Robert could not be sure. The emergency room at the hospital was not very busy so they took Henry right in and were able to give him the needed tests quickly and the best drugs on hand. The ER doctor told them it appeared to be quite a severe a stroke, but assured them that the staff would monitor him closely and there would be no need for them to stay. However, his mother insisted she would stay, so Robert, although quite shaken, returned to work and as soon as he could he phoned Terri to give her the sad news.

The news really shook Terri up because she loved Mr. Ewing as if he were her own father. She told Robert she wanted to go directly to the hospital after work so they agreed to meet at her house and both go in Robert's car.

Within the next four hours before quitting time and their visit to the hospital Mr. Ewing began to rally, no doubt the effect of the medication. It seemed that his whole left side was quite affected from the stroke. His speech was a little slurred, but the doctor told Edith that it would take 24 to 48 hours to really assess the damage. When Robert and Terri arrived they found that Mr. and Mrs. Rogers had already been there and left some flowers. No visitors were allowed for long in the room, and it was of little point to stay since Henry slept most of the time. Mrs. Ewing came with Robert and Terri to the coffee shop in the hospital as she had not had any lunch and was still too upset to be hungry. But they were able to sit and visit and attempt to comfort her.

Over the next couple of weeks it became evident that his father did have considerable damage that would require therapy with no guarantee that he would fully recover. The doctor said he should have some professional therapy for about three months at a proper live-in place and then it could be continued later at home depending on how his body responds. Henry could speak but was difficult to understand and was not able to use his left leg or arm much, but his mind was clear for which they were thankful. So Robert and his mother agreed with the doctor's suggestion and Henry was sent to the Winchester Rehabilitation Center by ambulance.

Now Robert and Terri were together quite a lot since they visited his father nearly every day and it gave them time together. The other brethren were very good at visiting Henry as well. Several of them took his mother to their home to supper in the weeks that followed, which eased the load on her, and they often included the young couple as well.

On one such visit to the senior Rogers home, Terri said to Mr. Rogers as they sat visiting, "Mr. Rogers, may I ask a question? I would like to remember the Lord Jesus at His Supper. What should I do?"

Mr. Rogers was surprised and paused a moment before answering, "That is a big commitment, Terri, I'm very pleased to hear that, and I'm sure that the Lord is greatly pleased. If that is truly your desire I will mention it to the other brethren. I'm sure they, too, will be pleased."

So it was several weeks later an announcement was to be made before the Lord's Supper that Terri would be breaking bread with them for the first time. She could hardly wait to express her love for her Savior in this way.

Henry Ewing was really cheered up when he heard of it and was so overjoyed that he began to weep. He had been praying for Terri to take the next step in her spiritual journey for a long time, and he had a lot of time to pray now. Terri went to him right away and put her arms around him in a long hug. He finally got control of himself and hugged Terri in a one-armed hug. "I am so pleased... I wish I could be there. I will be praying for you, Terri, that the Lord will give you a special portion."

That night sleep was out of the question, she read the accounts of the Lord's Supper in the Gospels of Matthew, Mark and Luke, and the section in John's Gospel that surrounded that time, and Paul's recounting of it in 1 Corinthians 11. Then she prayed and went over all that she had seen on each previous Lord's Day and also the explanations Robert had given her, until she finally fell asleep. When the alarm rang she was out of bed like a shot; she did not want to oversleep on this special hallowed day.

The day that she was to first remember the Lord dawned chilly and rainy, but it did not dampen her spirits. As she sat in her usual chair she was one of the first to arrive, since she was so anxious. The Scripture came to her mind about one arriving at the Lord's tomb *very early in the morning.* As she sat looking at the small table in the center of the room she thought of what she was going to do for the first time – take and eat a pinch of the bread and a sip of the cup (she thought it had either wine or grape juice in it), and by so doing she would show her love for the Lord Jesus. Of course, she had observed the Lord's Supper for many weeks, but today would be different.

When Mrs. Ewing sat down she placed her hand on Terri's arm with a reassuring squeeze. She was not exactly surprised that Edith came to the meeting, but it seemed so right even with the sadness and pressure she had been under, that the Lord Jesus was still first in her affections. *I need to learn that, even as much as I love Robert, Jesus must be first!*

The meeting proceeded like all the others she had been to, except this time as the loaf and the cup were passed to Mrs. Rogers, who sat on the other side of Terri, she passed them on to Terri. She could not help it, but her hands were shaking a little – it was a wonderful moment.

Yes, I have no question that the Lord has led me right. Robert thought, *What a blessing she already has been to us and now to the Lord.*

* * * * *

Terri was exhausted from all the excitement of the Lord's Day and when she got home she flopped down on her bed thinking she would just rest a minute before getting undressed. In a few seconds she was sound asleep.

It seemed like she had just fallen asleep when her mother burst into her room shouting, "Terri, Terri..." and then something she could not understand and when she turned on her light she realized her mother was drunk and dressed in a very skimpy nightie.

"What's wrong mom?"

Her mother aimed to sit on the edge of her bed but missed and crumpled to the floor. "There's sh-ome man... in my room! Get him..." and she could not finish the sentence.

"What man? Shall I call the police?"

"I don't know... do sh-ometing, Terri..." Her mother's words were very slurred.

"Mom you're drunk. Now get up and go to bed," she ordered.

Her mother moaned and mumbled something Terri could not understand like, "Where'sh my... my..." and her voice trailed off as she passed out.

So Terri was now fully awake so she disgustedly got up and realized she was still fully dressed so she began turning on lights; her bedroom, the hallway, and when she went to turn on the light in her mother's room there he was! Big as life lying on the floor! It scared Terri and she began to tremble; was he dead or alive?

It was *the lump* all right. She nudged him with her toe and he made no move at all, but she could hear him breathing so she knew he was alive. No way was she going to touch him, so she rushed back to her room. In the meantime her mother was still on the floor and was sound asleep. She decided the best thing was to call the police and then she would try to get some decent clothing on her mother.

After calling the police she ran downstairs and turned on the lights down there. Then back upstairs to dress her mother. Then back down because the police had arrived.

"Hello, thanks for coming. I don't know what to do. This guy my mother used to be friends with is passed out on her bedroom floor. They have been estranged for a while, but he must have had a key. Can you take him away."

"Let us have a look, Ma'am. Where is he?"

"Upstairs in her bedroom on the floor. I'll show you." She ran up the stairs with the two policemen following. She did not show them her mother. "I know he was uninvited because he had taken her car and left two weeks ago. His name is Dirk something, I think."

The men prodded him with their toe and he didn't move, but he was obviously breathing. "He is drunk, very drunk." The one officer said, "Do you want us to take him to the station and book him for trespassing?"

"Please, I cannot deal with him. He was never friendly to me."

"Where is your mother?" he inquired.

"She was drunk earlier in the evening and is sleeping now. I am quite sure she does not know he is here."

The one policeman produced a pad and began asking her questions; name, phone, mother's name, etc. Then the two officers hoisted him up and took him down the stairs.

When she shut the door and locked it she was so

relieved she nearly collapsed on the floor, but she still had her mother to deal with. Her final decision was to leave her mother where she was and go into the spare bedroom and attempt some sleep. She guessed all the kafuffle took about an hour that would make it about 2:00AM when it all started. Not much time for sleep before work.

When she awoke the next morning her mother was no longer in her room. She had gone back to her bed and was sleeping. So Terri quietly got ready for work without fixing her own lunch. She decided to go somewhere and buy lunch. She hated to think of the mess her mother had made of her life, but whenever she tried to talk sensibly with her she would not listen.

When she arrived at work she had a pounding headache and felt like she could fall asleep at any moment. Judy was her usual sarcastic self, especially about anything Christian. "Well, how did your religion go yesterday? I suppose just mah-velous," she made a mocking face.

"It went better than marvelous, Judy. But I hardly got any sleep because of mom and her... whatever you call him. I can't talk now, I'm too tired to think."

"OK!" And Judy went back to her workstation.

She got her computer started and her papers all lined up for the first visitor and then prayed there would be none. When she sat in her desk chair she could not see the front door but she told herself she would listen, then when she fell asleep Judy told her she had better talk to the boss and go home. And that is what she finally did, but she called Robert first and told him what had happened and asked him to call his mother and see if she could come there and sleep.

"Just a minute before you go…" Robert quickly said, "and I'll bring you my house key because mom most likely will be at the rehab place."

Robert was there very quickly and she was on her way to his home. It almost made her headache better just knowing she would not have to face the situation at her home. She wondered what the police would do with Dirk, but then she decided she didn't really care. She fell onto the sofa and was almost instantly asleep.

———

Chapter 18

Her mother had called her in the morning while she was still at work and asked what had happened. When she awoke she was in her bed with hardly any clothes on and her flimsy robe wrapped around. She was horrified when Terri told her what had happened and she started to cry.

"I'm dead tired, mom, and I'm going over to the Ewing's to sleep on their sofa this afternoon. I'm scared of that guy coming back again." Even her voice sounded groggy.

"I'm so sorry, honey. Call me later this afternoon to be sure I am all right; my head is pounding too," her mother sobbed out.

"OK, mom." *Huh? Mom's head is pounding... no wonder!*

At the Ewing's she got nearly 4 hours of really sound sleep and when she awoke she actually felt good, then read a few verses of Scripture and prayed. By the time she had her dress straightened up and her hair combed she heard the doorbell and discovered Robert was home from work.

When she opened the door he greeted her with a broad smile, "Well, did you get some sleep? Hope I didn't wake you." He said as he set his brief case down and took his coat off, "You still look just a bit frazzled. I had to ring because you have my key."

"Nope, I got up a few minutes ago. Oh, it was blissful! Everything was quiet and I did not even dream. Last night was enough of a nightmare for a long time."

Then he sat down and wanted to hear the full story and all that happened, which she recounted in detail. He was frightened for her.

"Rob, do you think I could stay here tonight yet? Do you think your mom would care? I'm scared to sleep at home. Hard telling where *the lump* is or what he will do."

"Hey, I think it's fine, but we will need to go to rehab anyhow, and we'll ask my folks. You could sleep in the spare bedroom." After a thoughtful pause, "We'll go to Rehab first, and then we can go to your house and you can pick up some clothes for tomorrow? Maybe we can find out what is going on with your mother."

"Good idea, I'll get my purse and then I'm ready."

At the rehab center it seemed that his father had made a bit of progress, although he was not very confident about walking. His speech even seemed a trifle better. When they asked about Terri staying over and told them what had happened they were agreeable since Edith would be there. Robert then told his mother that they were going to stop by the Nash's and pick up some clothes for Terri and that he was going to get Chinese carryout for dinner.

When Terri arrived at home to pick up her clothes Robert went in with her, because her mother's car was there and Terri was apprehensive of what she would find. Everything was hunky-dory, as they say. Dirk was ensconced in front of the TV but sound asleep, and her mother was doing something in the kitchen as happy as a lark, as if nothing had happened, and Terri was infuriated. To keep her up half the night with their drunkenness and then act as if there was nothing wrong... she could hardly keep her mouth shut. With Robert there she felt bolder, and went directly to her room without saying a word, and Robert stood by the front door watching *the lump* snoring away. Several cans of beer on the end table with a half spilled bag of Cheetos in his lap.

Soon Terri reappeared with her small case and called to her mother, "See ya' tomorrow."

"Where are you goin', honey?" Her mother called.

"The Ewing's have invited me to stay over there."

A dull, "Oh!" was all that came from the kitchen.

They stopped at Henry and Edith's favorite Chinese takeout restaurant and bought their dinner and by the time they got home to the Ewing's Robert's mother was already home with the table set for 3. They were pleased how Edith was holding up with the load that was on her. Henry was not getting better very quickly and they were all beginning to realize that he may never get back to where he was. It was an unspoken weight on them all.

* * * * *

"I've been thinking, honey, that maybe we could buy a house. We've been talking about so many things, but a house would be a good investment as well as someplace to start a family. What do you think?"

"That would be great!" Terri sighed, "But you know what? You have never asked me to marry you. Don't be so sure of yourself... Mr. Ewing!" Then she got a fit of embarrassed giggles.

"I don't believe it! I guess I just assumed it!"

"Well, what if I say 'No'?"

"Oh, no!" and Robert got down on one knee and took both her hands and said, in a mock formal tone of voice, "Terri Rachel Nash will you do me the honor of...?"

She was giggling so hard when she interrupted him that she nearly shouted, "YES!"

"You didn't let me finish," he was trying to keep a straight face.

"Well," and she had such a case of giggles she had to pause "you were going to ask me to marry you, right?"

"Now you spoiled it because I was going to ask if you would like to go to get some ice cream!" Of course, he was teasing and she knew it, but it took him a few seconds to realize that; "You knew I was teasing – I can never get ahead of you, you know that don't you?" She laughed till tears were rolling down her cheeks.

Being on the floor he just put his head in her lap and gave her a lopsided hug, "Fantastic! I love you Terri. Yes, let's celebrate!"

"I love you, Rob. Sorry I couldn't wait to say yes. We both were expecting this, but the excitement of it makes it so wonderful. Let's go tell your dad and mom after some ice cream. I want them to enjoy this as well, I love them so much."

They were so excited they each ordered a banana split but couldn't finish them. They chatted on about the plans they needed to make, especially about Robert's idea of buying a house. Wedding plans were also a subject; whom would they invite, and where should they have the wedding? Both their heads were spinning as they headed over to the Rehab center to see Robert's parents. They were quite sure Edith would still be there.

They literally burst through the door into Henry's room and sure enough Edith *was* still there and Terri ran to her future mother-in-law and hugged her all the while exclaiming, "We're getting married!" Henry attempted to stand from his wheel chair and hugged them both, and pronounced his blessing upon them and suggested that they pray together, which they did right then and there, all of them. Of course, they began talking about their plans, and in the middle of it Terri produced her father's letter and read it to them. Reading it again was good because Terri had already forgotten parts of it. Everyone was visibly moved by it.

* * * * *

After their engagement excitement and they were back home at the Ewing's house Robert said, "As I mentioned before, I've been kicking around this idea of buying a house and have been saving all I possibly can and was hoping to get enough for a down payment. I hate the idea of paying rent because in the end you have nothing. I think my parents might help us out for the down payment. My job pays well so I don't think we would have a problem getting a mortgage. Next time we are at the Rehab center let's ask my folks for some input. What do you say?"

"Yes, good idea! I guess I hadn't got that far in my plans." She exclaimed.

Snuggled up together on the sofa in the Ewing's lower level was their favorite place to be. They both enjoyed talking; they talked about Biblical things as well as every other subject under the sun. They found that they both liked children and would like a family if it pleased the Lord to give it.

"I want to stay at home, if I can, and give my children all the love and attention that I never had, and I don't want to marry a man who'll be any different than you! All I remember as a child was the need to grow up so I could find some friends and travel and have my own fun. I definitely did not want to marry a wealthy man and live like my grandparents. As a child everything I knew of them I hated! Sure, he might have made his money from the Nash automobile, but where did it get him? Fortunately, or unfortunately I only saw them two or three times. Isn't it horrible to grow up that way, and now as I learn about the family of God... what a contrast!" Robert sat quietly listening.

She went on, "Am I unreasonable in this?" She asked as she turned so she could face him. "After what happened at my grandparents, and the way they ignored me and spoke nasty to me, I don't ever want any child of mine to face anything like that. I suppose your childhood was so different," she paused so Robert could speak.

"As you were telling me all this it made me feel so sad. To think of someone I love going through something like that, and as a child too. No, my childhood was not at all like that. I can remember grandpa crawling around on the floor with a scary bearskin rug draped over him to scare me. See, my mother had some problem after I was born and could have no more children. I think they talked about adopting, but then felt that if it was God's will they have only one child they would accept that, but it was hard, especially for mom.

"My uncle and aunt, dad's brother, had six children, but we seldom saw them since Uncle Sid married a woman from the world and left the fellowship. They still live in Akron, Ohio and don't go to any church, as far as we know, and since we were poor and they were poor we seldom got together." Robert took her hand and held it, then "but we will always have each other!"

* * * * *

So several evenings later they mentioned the idea of buying a house to Henry and Edith while they were all gathered in Henry's room. His parents were pleased at being included in such plans. So Robert took out a notepad and began to jot down a rough financial plan with input from his parents and Terri. His father's speech was still very slurred but his mind was sharp. It certainly was not going to be a joy ride financially, but it appeared they should explore the possibility of getting a mortgage.

So the next Saturday morning Robert went to the bank where he and his parents had their accounts. Mr. M'Ginty was most kind and helpful and when he looked at the numbers Robert had written down he said he felt it was very likely that Robert could get the loan he needed. Robert was so elated with the news that he headed right over to Terri's house to talk with her.

Since her mother and Dirk were not home they sat on the sofa to talk. He told her what the banker had said and that he had given him papers to fill out to get pre-approved for a mortgage. So the next thing was for them to contact a realtor to see what houses were available. They were both very excited and decided to set aside the following Saturday for house hunting, but they never got to do it.

In all the upset with Robert's father and his stroke and then going into rehab, plus all of their rejoicing that Terri was now remembering the Lord in the Lord's Supper they had forgotten, well, not exactly forgotten; no, not that at all, but they had had no time to go shopping for an engagement ring.

"First things first" Robert said, "we've got to go ring hunting before house hunting! Let's go Saturday."

By that Saturday the excitement had been building

in Terri all night long, so that she had hardly slept. *Wow, this will make it official and for certain – I am about to get married.* It turned out to be an especially nice day for early March, it was overcast but not raining. They went to several jewelers to check out prices as neither one of them knew what to expect. Terri did not want to spend a lot because she wanted to save for a house, but Robert wanted a very nice ring. He wanted it to be a diamond. He said it would be a reminder of their love for years to come.

Finally, after visiting several shops they made the big decision and bought a ring. Terri was so elated she could hardly keep from dancing.

"Oh, Rob, I love it! I love it! It is over-the-top gorgeous! Even if it only had a pebble in it I would love it because you gave it to me."

Right there in the store Robert took her left hand in his and placed the ring on the proper finger and drew her into his arms and, yes, their lips met for a long time. They clung together for a long kiss and they both savored the moment. They were engaged for everyone to see, and proud of it.

When they were back in the car Robert brought Terri out of her reverie with his statement, "Next we need to pick a date so that plans can be made, and your father can be notified. I sure would like him to be there."

All the way to his father's rehab center they kicked around ideas for a date for the wedding. They wanted to postpone it a few months in hopes his father could be part of it too, so it looked like June was the best choice. That would make it about 3 months away, and hopefully Henry would be more recovered by then.

Henry and Edith both thought the ring was most "becoming" and beautiful and they congratulated the couple again. Henry said they should not postpone the wedding on account of him, and Terri spoke up immediately and told him that she really wanted him there and that she thought June was the best time. So June the 17th was the chosen date.

"Thank you for all your help and encouragement! I would like to call you 'Dad' and 'Mom' even though we are not married yet? You both mean so much to me." Then a tear ran down her cheek as she went to Henry and hugged him.

"Yes, you may, *daughter*!" He said in his slurred way, but his eyes said he was elated.

As she hugged Edith they both had wet eyes.

The couple decided to leave as Henry was already getting tired, so they went and had another Starbucks and spent the afternoon together driving to nowhere in particular, after which they had pizza for supper.

The ring felt funny, or rather unusual on her finger. She kept twirling it around and around with her thumb and sleep was out of the question for a long time, but she refused to take the ring off for any reason. She remembered her mother telling her never to wear any ring on that finger until she was engaged – "it makes the engagement very special," *for once mom was right.*

———————

Chapter 19

During the last week of April the weather had been unseasonably beautiful all week long and on Friday Robert phoned Terri and asked if she would like to go see The Falls on Saturday. He suggested they leave in the mid-morning and take a picnic lunch, and then have dinner.

"I would like to go up in the Skylon Tower where we can get a great view of everything, and there is a restaurant there too. The tower is quite new so I've never gone up there before," he suggested.

"Wow, that sounds exciting," she said over the phone.

"I'll take care of getting the lunch packed and I'll pick you up at about nine o'clock. Is that OK?"

"Yes, fine."

Terri had only stayed at the Ewing's the one night several weeks before, but things seem to have settled back into the usual routine with her mom and Dirk. She still kept her door locked now that Dirk was around again. This would be great to get away for a day just the two of them.

As she slid into the car Saturday morning and greeted Robert she exclaimed, "Guess what? I got a letter from dad yesterday and he said he was putting our wedding date into his schedule so he doesn't forget. I am really excited about seeing him. I wonder what he will look like?"

"That is wonderful, Terri. It is really great that you have reconnected with him even if it is by letter only so far. Hopefully he doesn't have the same problem your mom does with drink."

The drive to Niagara did not take long at all, and especially as they were talking the whole time. It seemed the wedding was what they mostly talked about. Planning, planning, "It's a good thing we're not having a big bash." Robert said.

"I'm glad it will be small. On my side of the family the only two I want there are my parents – if my mom will even come. Dirk is definitely un-invited! I told mom this and she did not like it, so I said 'too bad!'"

"I doubt if he would even want to come except to spite you. There will be no alcoholic drinks served and many of your old friends would find that a turn-off."

"I guess the time from now on will fly, but it can't go fast enough for me. I want moved out of the rat's nest I live in!"

"Is that why you want to marry me, just so you can move?" Robert teased and laughed.

"Of course, you are no plum yourself, you know!" She teased back. So they had a good laugh, but just then they had to find a parking place at the falls.

As they walked up to the overlook Terri was stunned. She had never seen so much water in all her life, and to think it kept coming and coming.

"Won't it ever run out of water?" She asked.

"I don't think it ever has, although I think it has frozen up a time or two and the water has stopped. I understand it woke all the people living nearby when it stopped. They were so used to the continual roar."

"I just can't believe it, and it is so beautiful! It makes my hands sweaty just to think of someone stupid enough to try going over in a barrel or something." Terri just stared and stared.

"Do you want to ride on the 'Maid of the Mist'? That's that boat down there." Robert said as he pointed down to the river.

"If you want to, of course, I am just fine with standing here."

"I want to take a picture. Could you stand over here and give me one of those million dollar smiles of yours?"

"Only if I can use your camera next!"

"It's very complex and takes a very smart person to use it. I doubt you can handle it." *There he goes teasing again!*

"Well, Mr. Smarty Pants, you'll just see what I can do with that 'complex' thing. You can give me a frown if you want and I will still love the picture." She was six to his half dozen!

The roaring falls made a beautiful backdrop for their pictures. Just as they turned to go down to the boat another visitor asked Robert, "Would you like me to take one of the two of you?"

"That would be very kind of you," and Robert smiled as he handed him his camera. That done they finally got to the boat, and what a view it was from that low vantage point. When the boat ride was finished it was approaching suppertime so they headed to the tower.

The Skylon Tower was awesome. The elevator ride to the sky deck was even an experience in itself, but the view from the top was fantastic. They both enjoyed it, and Robert clicked quite a few pictures.

"Look at that Robert," Terri said pointing down, "we are even higher than the eagles. See that one circling down there?"

"When you sit like this it is better than being in a plane because you are not so high up. It reminds me of the Scripture that speaks about those of us that trust in God, *'they shall mount up with wings as eagles'*"

They were pleased to get a table right next to the window, and as they ate they saw a beautiful sunset. But the sunset signaled it was time to go home. It had been a wonderful day for both of them. The trip home was of two tired people who had done a lot, seen a lot, and talked a lot. So Robert walked her to the door and gave her a goodnight hug.

"Thank you, Rob, for a wonderful day. See you in the morning."

"Goodnight, sweetheart!"

* * * * *

The six weeks before the wedding went by faster than they expected because they were filled with things that had to be done. Robert's father was gaining a little and would perhaps be able to walk with help. Edith wanted a lot of cleaning done at the house and the flower gardens planted with petunias, marigolds, and many other colorful flowers. Both Robert and Terri worked together to get it done. Windows were washed; the carpets cleaned, the bathrooms scrubbed, and on and on went the list. They worked evenings when there were no meetings and every Saturday. Terri often fell into bed exhausted, because she had her own chores to do at home.

One weekend shortly after they had gone to Niagara Falls Edith told Terri she would go with her to get a wedding dress if she would like because Henry said he wanted to pay for it. What an experience that was! She and Edith spent quite a lot of time in several wedding shops until they found a dress that was just right. Her mother-in-law had helped her find a beautiful white wedding dress that was modest and yet looked gorgeous on her.

There were no young people in Rochester that were old enough to be witnesses for the wedding so Terri asked Sadie, whom she met at the Hamilton meetings, who lived in St. Catherines, to be her bridesmaid. Robert had asked Ronald to be his best man, but he declined because Alyssa was pregnant and he would have to help with Peter. So he asked a good friend from Gault, Ontario – Jonathan to be best man – both attendants were from Canada, yet not far away.

Both Terri and Robert wanted a small wedding and accordingly did not invite many, of course, all the brethren from their small meeting were invited. She invited her mother and her father, as well as Judy from work. At the last minute Robert thought they should invite his uncle from Ohio and his family thinking it might be good to try to re-establish their links.

One black family from New York had asked to come, so they were included, as were Alyssa's parents and another family from Chicago. But the numbers would not be large, because with Henry in the rehab center there had been extra expense and they needed to keep the cost down. And Terri was always thinking of the funds they would need for a house. Not just the cost of the house but something to sit on and sleep on. She certainly was not an extravagant girl, but still it would cost money.

Henry was released from rehab on the first of June and managed to settle in fairly well at home. The bedroom he and Edith used was on the first floor so he never had to negotiate stairs unless he went out, which they would be doing for the wedding. He was

———————

now able to walk slowly using a walker and some extra help.

Chapter 20

The appointed Saturday in June was a beautiful day, although quite warm. The wedding was to start in the early afternoon to give some of those coming from afar time to drive. Terri's father agreed to walk with her into the meeting room and she was very pleased. There would be no pageantry, such as music playing, etc. They had worried that there would be too many to fit in their meeting room, but after several careful counts of those expected to be there they concluded it would work. They rented 50 additional folding chairs and set them up plus their own chairs in auditorium style. Ronald was a great help with all this. They left just enough space at the front of the room for Mr. Adams to stand facing the young couple and their attendants. The plan was to have the meeting to follow immediately after the ceremony and then allow a short time to greet the new Mr. & Mrs. Robert Ewing. Then they would adjourn to a nearby park for a few photos.

Mr. Adams was able to perform the legal part of the wedding as well as being a well-respected brother in their meeting. Under state law he was able to perform weddings because he was a preacher of the gospel. Robert and Terri wanted him to not only say "until death do us part" but to add-in the words "or until the Lord Jesus comes for us," which he was pleased to do. So the actual marriage ceremony went very well. Terri especially liked the part where he said to

Robert, "You may kiss your wife."

They had asked Ronald Rogers to make the needed announcements, so after their vows were said he walked to front of the room and announced, "We would like everyone to remain seated and we will proceed with the meeting, and then you may congratulate the couple."

Four seats had been reserved in front for the wedding party and they sat there. And the small podium was moved to the center in front. Then Mr. Rogers gave a short word and so did Mr. Cunningham from Chicago (Alyssa's father), both encouraging the young couple to put the Lord first in their marriage and their eventual home. When the meeting concluded everyone was eager to speak, kiss, and hug the bride and groom.

By prior arrangement the photographer arrived and everyone adjourned to the park for a photo session. It was a beautiful day and the flowers were at their prime. The photographer, Elaine, was really good at composing various shots. The one with Robert's parents was arranged so his father could be seated on a decorative stone to avoid the wheelchair.

After the photo session it would be time for dinner. Robert had made reservations at the Dutch Windmill Restaurant, a large restaurant where they could have a private dining room. This worked out very well and the menu of roast beef, mashed potatoes, and some vegetables was very tasty and enjoyed by everyone.

When the meal was finished Ronald announced,

"The Ewing's would like for everyone to be free to come to their home for a short visit. The parents of the bride and groom have asked me to thank you all for coming; we feel the Lord has blessed the time. I would like to suggest that perhaps Mr. Ewing might conclude this occasion with a prayer?" And as he turned to Henry and quietly said, "We can help you to stand if you like." Everyone looked surprised but pleased at Ronald's suggestion. Ronald and Robert both hurried to Robert's father's side and held him as he struggled to stand. It took several long seconds before he could speak; he was very emotionally moved to have the opportunity to thank the Lord for all His blessings. Terri was unashamedly moved to shed some tears, happy tears.

Robert's father had done better than they had expected. Terri and Robert drove in Robert's car so they could transport Kenneth, her father; while Edith and Henry drove by themselves. Terri's mother surprised them by saying she would like to come to the house as well, and Terri was very pleased; pleased that both her mother and father could see her new family and hopefully in time come to know her Savior.

When they got to the house Terri's father hugged her a long time and whispered, "I am so pleased about your wedding, Terri. I think Robert is a real prize! I hope you two have a long and happy married life.

"I have booked to fly home on Monday evening, and I hope I can have some time with you both tomorrow and Monday morning, that is, if you are not going on your honeymoon right away."

"We planned on having time with you before leaving, and I am so looking forward to doing some catch-up." Terri enthused.

The evening at the Ewing's home went very well and everyone seemed to have a good time. The couple got many very nice gifts. As usual some useful and some not so useful, but they were grateful for all the love expressed. What was most shocking was the letter from Terri's father which he handed to Terri at the house.

Dear Robert and Terri,

Congratulations on your marriage! I hope you will have a long and wonderful life together. However, there will be the usual difficulties, which I have found and am ashamed of, but I hope you will be able to work through them. Remember, money cannot buy love.

As a gift for you I am prepared to buy you a house, which you can make into a home. It is for you to choose and let me know when you have found it.

I hope to be a visitor many times.

My much love to you both,

Dad

After Robert read it aloud Terri just covered her face with her hands and cried, she was so excited. She threw her arms around her father and hugged him all the while thanking him over and over again.

And almost as astonishing was an envelope he handed to Muriel, and when she opened it he had written his apologies for the years past and said he wanted to begin proceedings to pay off the mortgage on her home as soon as he could. She broke down and wept and when she could speak she said, "Thank you, Kenneth, you really don't need to do this."

"I really want to do this, there are no strings attached. I'll have my lawyer contact you soon."

When everyone had left the house, Robert asked her father, "Which hotel did you book into?"

"I'm staying at the Hilton downtown."

"Great that's the same one Terri and I are staying at. We'll drive you there if you want," Robert interjected.

"That'll be swell." Kenneth then thanked Henry and Edith for such a nice time and said he hoped Henry would recover fully. He complimented them on raising such a wonderful son and how pleased he was with the marriage.

And they thanked him for coming, and Henry said, "It meant a lot to Terri. We are glad you and she can reconnect. She was so excited to receive your letters. You have a wonderful daughter!"

On the way to the hotel Robert and Terri told him they would be going to the Lord's Supper in the morning.

"Would I be allowed to go with you to that meeting? I'll just sit in back in some corner and observe." Ken asked hesitantly.

"Of course! We have no secret meetings." Robert was really pleased that he asked and pleased for Terri's sake, since he knew it would mean a lot to her.

They discussed a time to meet for breakfast before going to the meeting, and then how the rest of their day would be spent. Kenneth wanted to spend time talking with them and catching up on Terri's life.

The visit of Terri's father in some ways overshadowed their wedding, but they both felt it was a rare opportunity to share their faith with him. Especially since he was to their wedding meeting and then, beyond Terri's expectation, he had come to the Lord's Supper. Terri's emotions were on overload. All of this with her father after so many years, and then being married to the man she loved. She was excited and "giddy" and overwhelmed all at once.

Neither of them slept much on their wedding night. It

was so awesome to finally share the same the same bed... They were both *dead* tired and yet they had so much to share with each other. There was no doubt that their married life was starting out with a bang and they were loving it!

Although Robert had not known her father he liked him at once, and especially how tender and loving he was to Terri. Whatever pleased Terri pleased Robert. He kept wanting to pinch himself to be sure it was real – *I am married to the sweetest, most caring and beautiful girl in the whole world... unbelievable!*

After breakfast Monday morning Kenneth asked them to come to his room – or rather his suite – so they could visit. It was clear he was a man used to the finer things in life.

"You know that letter I gave you about buying a house... I was not kidding. Now don't go overboard you'll need something you can afford in an ongoing basis, but please don't skimp on account of me. You can buy a mansion if you want, but the maintenance and upkeep will be expensive." Turning to Terri, "all these years I have not been there for you, I feel I owe it to you, and I can well afford it. So, Robert, I want you to get busy house hunting and let me know when you have decided on a place. I'll be happy to counsel you if you like, but it is completely your decision. Then my lawyer will work with you, or with your lawyer, and get it done."

Terri was almost overcome with appreciation, "Daddy, you are wonderful! I want to make up all those years we lost. We need to keep close this time."

Robert interjected, "We don't know what to say about such a gift. It is certainly something we will never forget and just to say 'thank you' seems inadequate. It was also very kind of you to give Terri's mom such a generous gift."

"Well, Robert, when I stand before the Righteous Judge I want to be clear of any hindrance to blessing. We should never have quarreled and I should not have done what I did, but it seems it cannot be changed now."

"If you have put your faith and trust in the Lord Jesus Christ and in His sacrifice for sin, then you are, in the eyes of God, righteous because of Jesus, and there is no charge before God. Have you ever done this, Dad? If I may call you that?" Robert ventured.

"I love being called that by you. You now own one of the sweetest things in my life. To answer your other question… I can't say I have done it quite that clearly. I just sort of always thought that I was OK. I realized Jesus had died for sin, but I don't think… as I think back now… that I ever really had any transaction with Him directly."

Terri exclaimed, "I had hardly ever seen a Bible until I saw Robert reading his. Then I told him I thought it was all a mixture of history, fairy tales and legends. What you don't know is that my life was spiraling out of control before I met Robert. When I came directly to Jesus Himself what a difference He made. I found a level of peace and joy in my heart that I never thought possible to have. Maybe you could find that." At this moment she handed him a Bible she had bought for him, a very nice one!

"Thank you, sweetheart. I will begin to read it. Should I start at the beginning?"

"I would suggest you start in John's Gospel. I think Terri put the ribbon in there," Robert joined in.

"I promise you I will do that. Now for some lunch and you two can take me to the airport. I'm off for Paris,

France tomorrow, but I will be carrying a Bible this time!"

"Do you have to travel much?" Terri asked.

"Yes, quite a bit. We have offices in 12 foreign countries. This time I have a messy problem in Paris to attend to, so I will betaking the Concorde in the early morning. I will arrive in Paris and see to the problem and have lunch and board the Concorde for New York. I have a supper engagement with the New York mayor at 7:00 PM. You can bet I will be tired after that!"

"Wow, I'd no idea that you would have to do all that. I am worried that you will over-do it and have a heart attack," she cautioned.

"I'll try, but some things just can't be avoided... love ya' both," and after hugs and kisses he walked into the airport terminal building and was gone.

They both were pleased with their visit with her father and felt they had laid some groundwork that might lead to his salvation. And what a gift he had given them – stunned was the only word they could think of. So now they would have to really begin to hunt for a house.

"This week is all ours... just you and I, sweetheart. Let's not think of anything at home."

"Yeah, nobody else!" She cooed as she scooted over closer to him in the front seat of the car, and gave him a peck on the cheek.

THE END

The author welcomes you comments by email --

w.s.c@sbcglobal.net

Here are some other books you might also like.

You might also,

enjoy Courtnee's story. She is a sweet 10 year old Amish girl who has normal growing pains and experiences and learns many good lessons. One is learning to quilt from her grandmother.
She becomes very good friends with an English (not Amish) girl quite by accident. Her community is a very interesting place. Her story is told in these 4 books called the

"Farm Girl Series"

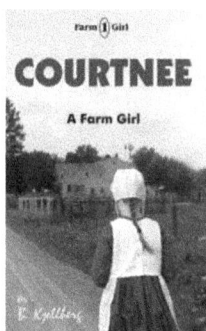

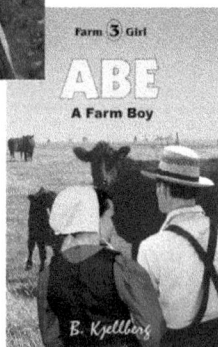

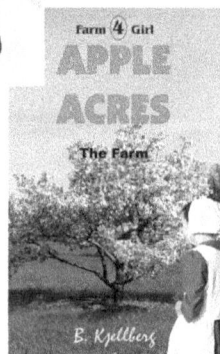

Order from:
The author at --
w.s.c@sbcglobal.net

The story of
one of the most
Amazing Women in Christian History

Devoted!

Selina the Countess of Huntingdon

One of the wealthiest women in the 1700s and she spent her entire fortune on the support of the gospel and the preachers.

It is historically correct except the conversations have been fictionalized. Her history is truly one to challenge any reader.

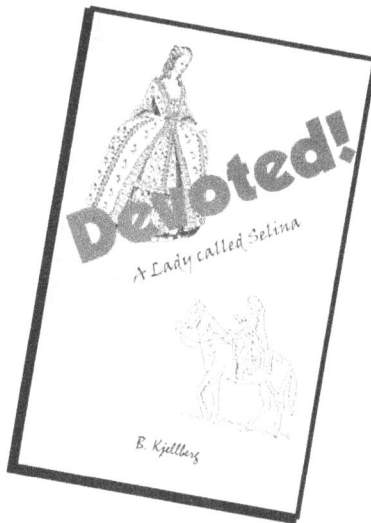

Devoted!
A Lady called Selina

B. Kjellberg

Order from:
w.s.c@sbcglobal.net